100 Days of Blessing

Devotions for Wives and Mothers

Volume 1

Nancy Campbell

Prescott Publishing

Above Rubies
PO Box 681687
Franklin TN 37068-1687
www.aboverubies.org

Printed in cooperation with Prescott Publishing
http://prescottpublishing.org

ISBN: 978-0-9826-2696-2

All Scriptures used in this book are from the King James Version or Revised Authorized Version (which is practically the same as the King James Version, except for "thee" and "thou"). Other translations mentioned and abbreviated in the text are as follows:

CJB	Complete Jewish Bible
GNB	Good News Bible
JPB	The New Testament translated by J. B. Phillips
KNOX	The Holy Bible translated by Monsignor Knox
MSG	The Message
MLB	Modern Language Bible
NASB	New American Standard Bible
NEB	New English Bible
NIV	New International Version
NLT	New Living Translation
RSV	Revised Standard Version
TLB	The Living Bible

Cover Design: Kelly Barnes
Email: kellvers@yahoo.com

Kelly's inspiration for the cover: The stairs show the steps we take to lead us closer to God and the blessings He has for us. The stone speaks of the strength God gives to wives and mothers. We may get "weathered" over the years, but it only makes us more beautiful. God created us with an inner strength to be the solid, nurturing, support for our families. The flowers remind us of God and His creation. While we can be strong, it is only through Him we can make the journey. The lace wraps the book around, just as God wraps us in His unfailing love. While the stairs show our strength, the lace reveals our femininity, grace, and softer side.

For the mothers of the world, for whom I
give my life as a "labor of love."

Contents

Introduction 1

Day 1   Always Abounding 3

Day 2   Good Workmanship 5

Day 3   The Joyful Life 7

Day 4   God Is Still With You 9

Day 5   A Prikly Pear? 11

Day 6   My Miracles 13

Day 7   A Happy Face 15

Day 8   All The Days Of My Life 17

Day 9   One, Two, Three Go! 19

Day 10   My Resting Place 21

Day 11   Above Only, Part 1 24

Day 12   Above Only, Part 2 26

Day 13   Above Only, Part 3 28

Day 14   The Right Questions 30

Day 15   Are You Kind? 32

Day 16   Goodies And Baddies 34

Day 17   Queen Of Your Home, Part 1 36

Day 18   Queen Of Your Home, Part 2 38

Day 19   Queen Of Your Home, Part 3 40

Day 20   The Nurturing Anointing .42

Day 21   Town Or Country 45

Day 22   I Am Dangerous 47

Day 23   My Mission Field 50

Day 24   Are You Up Or Down? Part 1 52

Day 25   Are You Up Or Down? Part 2 54

Day 26   Are You Up Or Down? Part 3A 56

Day 27   Are You Up Or Down? Part 3B 58

Day 28   Are You Up Or Down? Part 3C 60

Day 29   Are You Up Or Down? Part 4 62

Day 30   Tinkling With Joy 64

Day 31   Wear The Right Clothes 66

Day 32   Bigger Than You! 68

Day 33   Born To Look Up 70

Day 34   Me Brutish? Surely Not! 72

Day 35   Which Camp? 74

Day 36   Choices Have Consequences 76

Day 37   Covenant Keepers, Part 1 78
Day 38   Covenant Keepers, Part 2 80
Day 39   God's Handmaiden. 82
Day 40   Don't Give In To Doubt. 84
Day 41   Enough Hours In The Day? 86
Day 42   Don't Waste Brain Space 88
Day 43   Family Togetherness. 90
Day 44   Feminine Power, Part 1. 92
Day 45   Feminine Power, Part 2. 95
Day 46   Feminine Power, Part 3. 97
Day 47   The "Filled" Word, Part 1 99
Day 48   Keep On Being Filled, Part 2 102
Day 49   Keep On Being Filled, Part 3 104
Day 50   Keep On Being Filled, Part 4 106
Day 51   Keep On Being Filled, Part 5 108
Day 52   Keep On Being Filled, Part 6 110
Day 53   Follow The Leader 112
Day 54   Free To Be You! 114
Day 55   Pay Them Back, Part 1 116
Day 56   Pay Them Back, Part 2 118
Day 57   Pay Them Back, Part 3 120
Day 58   Leave Your Problems At The Door. .122
Day 59   God Comes Down 124
Day 60   What Do You Fear? 126
Day 61   God Is Close To The Broken-Hearted 128
Day 62   Power For Patience. 130
Day 63   Hasty Words. 132
Day 64   Hold On To Your Crown 134
Day 65   God Knows Your Sorrows 136
Day 66   It's Not As Bad As You Think 138
Day 67   Have You Dedicated Your Home? Part 1 140
Day 68   Have You Dedicated Your Home? Part 2 142
Day 69   Have You Dedicated Your Home? Part 3 144
Day 70   Don't Look Around—Look Up!. 147
Day 71   How's Your Self-Control?. 149
Day 72   Home Destroyers, Part 1 151
Day 73   Home Destroyers, Part 2A 153
Day 74   Home Destroyers, Part 2B 155
Day 75   Home Destroyers, Part 3 158
Day 76   Home Destroyers, Part 4 160

Day 77   Home Destroyers, Part 5 163
Day 78   Is Your Home A Lighthouse? 166
Day 79   You Gotta Learn To Wait! 168
Day 80   Lasting Treasures 171
Day 81   Leaning On Jesus 173
Day 82   The Comforts Of Sterility 175
Day 83   Which Language? 177
Day 84   Your Testimony 179
Day 85   Godly Children 181
Day 86   I Need Strength! 183
Day 87   Enemy Chasers 186
Day 88   The Warmth Of A Smile 188
Day 89   Faint, Yet Pursuing 190
Day 90   It's Futile 193
Day 91   Bypath Meadow 195
Day 92   It Takes A Turning 197
Day 93   Dress For The Job! 199
Day 94   Cling To The Lord 201
Day 95   The Saddest Question! 203
Day 96   My Highest Purpose, Part 1 205
Day 97   My Highest Purpose, Part 2 207
Day 98   My Highest Purpose, Part 3 209
Day 99   The Door Of Hope 211
Day 100   Enrich Your Home 213
Affirmations For You To Pin Up In Your Home 215
Further Information and Study 218

Alphabetical Contents

Introduction 1
Day 11   Above Only, Part 1 24
Day 12   Above Only, Part 2 26
Day 13   Above Only, Part 3 28
Day 7   A Happy Face. 15
Day 8   All The Days Of My Life 17
Day 1   Always Abounding. 3
Day 5   A Prickly Pear? 11
Day 15   Are You Kind? 32
Day 24   Are You Up Or Down? Part 1 52
Day 25   Are You Up Or Down? Part 2 54
Day 26   Are You Up Or Down? Part 3A .56
Day 27   Are You Up Or Down? Part 3B .58
Day 28   Are You Up Or Down? Part 3C .60
Day 29   Are You Up Or Down? Part 4 62
Day 32   Bigger Than You! 68
Day 33   Born To Look Up. 70
Day 91   Bypath Meadow 195
Day 36   Choices Have Consequences 76
Day 94   Cling To The Lord 201
Day 37   Covenant Keepers, Part 1 78
Day 38   Covenant Keepers, Part 2 80
Day 40   Don't Give Into Doubt. 84
Day 70   Don't Look Around—Look Up!. 147
Day 42   Don't Waste Brain Space 88
Day 93   Dress For The Job! 199
Day 87   Enemy Chasers. 186
Day 41   Enough Hours In The Day? 86
Day 100 Enrich Your Home. 213
Day 89   Faint, Yet Persuing 190
Day 43   Family Togetherness. 90
Day 44   Feminine Power, Part 1. 92
Day 45   Feminine Power, Part 2. 95
Day 46   Feminine Power, Part 3. 97
Day 53   Follow The Leader 112
Day 54   Free To Be You! 114
Day 59   God Comes Down 124

Day 61	God Is Close To The Broken-Hearted	128
Day 4	God Is Still With You	9
Day 65	God Knows Your Sorrows	136
Day 85	Godly Children?	181
Day 39	Gods Handmaiden	82
Day 16	Goodies And Baddies	34
Day 2	Good Workmanship	5
Day 63	Hasty Words	132
Day 67	Have You Dedicated Your Home? Part 1	140
Day 68	Have You Dedicated Your Home? Part 2	142
Day 69	Have You Dedicated Your Home? Part 3	144
Day 64	Hold On To Your Crown	134
Day 72	Home Destroyers, Part 1	151
Day 73	Home Destroyers, Part 2A	153
Day 74	Home Destroyers, Part 2B	155
Day 75	Home Destroyers, Part 3	158
Day 76	Home Destroyers, Part 4	160
Day 77	Home Destroyers, Part 5	163
Day 71	How's Your Self-Control?	149
Day 22	I Am Dangerous	47
Day 86	I Need Strength!	183
Day 78	Is Your Home A Lighthouse?	166
Day 92	It Takes A Turning	197
Day 90	It's Futile	193
Day 66	It's Not As Bad As You Think	138
Day 47	The "Filled" Word, Part 1	99
Day 48	Keep On Being Filled, Part 2	102
Day 49	Keep On Being Filled, Part 3	104
Day 50	Keep On Being Filled, Part 4	106
Day 51	Keep On Being Filled, Part 5	108
Day 52	Keep On Being Filled, Part 6	110
Day 80	Lasting Treasures	171
Day 81	Leaning On Jesus	173
Day 58	Leave Your Problems At The Door	122
Day 34	Me Brutish? Surely Not!	72
Day 96	My Highest Purpose, Part 1	205
Day 97	My Highest Purpose, Part 2	207
Day 98	My Highest Purpose, Part 3	209
Day 6	My Miracles	13
Day 23	My Mission Field	50

Day 10   My Resting Place 21
Day 9   One, Two, Three Go!. 19
Day 55   Pay Them Back, Part 1 116
Day 56   Pay Them Back, Part 2 118
Day 57   Pay Them Back, Part 3 120
Day 62   Power For Patience. 130
Day 17   Queen Of Your Home, Part 1. .36
Day 18   Queen Of Your Home, Part 2. .38
Day 19   Queen Of Your Home, Part 3. .40
Day 30   Tinkling With Joy 64
Day 82   The Comforts Of Sterility 175
Day 99   The Door Of Hope. 211
Day 3   The Joyful Life 7
Day 20   The Nuturing Anointing. 42
Day 14   The Right Questions. 30
Day 95   The Saddest Question! 203
Day 88   The Warmth Of A Smile 188
Day 21   Town Or Country. 45
Day 31   Wear The Right Clothes. 66
Day 60   What Do You Fear? 126
Day 35   Which Camp? 74
Day 83   Which Language?. 177
Day 79   You Gotta Learn To Wait! 168
Day 84   Your Testimony. 179
Catchphrases. 215
Further Study 218

Introduction

I pray that God will minister to you mightily as you read these devotions. Some will comfort you; others will challenge you. This is what the Word of God does to us as we read it with expectation—it both comforts and challenges.

These devotions are not the average daily thought for women. They will refresh and enlarge your vision. They are meaty and will give you strength for your great and noble task of training and mothering the next generation. You are doing the greatest job in the nation and you need a double dose of God's strength. The greatest way to receive new vitality each day is from God's precious Word which fortifies and builds you up.

I have written a prayer at the end of each devotion. It is a cry that comes from my own heart. Pray it with me. You may want to pray it out loud which is far more powerful than praying silently.

Don't forget to confess out loud the affirmation, too. There is nothing like affirming the Word. 1 Corinthians 4:13 states, "*I believe, therefore have I spoken.*" We receive Christ by believing in our heart that Jesus Christ died and rose again and by confessing with our mouth that Jesus is Lord (Romans 10:9-10). We now continue our walk with God the same way—believing and confessing. It is not enough to believe. We must also confess and affirm the truth. Therefore, speak the affirmation out loud, not once, but twice, or even three times!

You will most probably want to read the devotions consecutively each day. What do you do when you come to the end? Start again. You will not be able to imbibe the revelation of these devotions in one reading. You'll be ready to read them again when you finish. Sometimes you may want to read a particular devotion because it is what you are going through at the moment.

You will notice this is Volume 1. Volume 2 is also published and Volumes 3 and 4 will be published later.

May God bless you, Nation Builder! May these devotions strengthen you in your great vocation.

NANCY CAMPBELL
Primm Springs, Tennessee USA
www.aboverubies.org

Day 1

Always Abounding

*"Therefore, my beloved brethren, be ye steadfast, unmovable,
always abounding in the work of the Lord, forasmuch as ye know
that your labor is not in vain in the Lord"*
(1 Corinthians 15:58).

What is the greatest work you can do for the Lord as a mother? Of course, there is no greater ministry than mothering and caring for the needs of your children. God has given your precious children to you to nurture and train on His behalf! He is your Employer! Be encouraged and don't grow weary in well doing.

God doesn't want you to only "do" your mothering ministry, but to "abound" in it. I checked the word "abounding" in the Greek Lexicon and was amazed to see the depth of meaning. It means "to super-abound, to excel, to exceed, to increase, be in excess, be better, more abundant, enough and to spare." It comes from a root word that means, "sense of beyond, to go beyond what is necessary, superabundant in quantity and superior in quality." This is how we are to mother; not half-heartedly, but with all our might! To do more than is necessary! To go the second mile! To aim for excellence!

This is the challenge, but there is also a promise! God promises that our mothering ministry will not be in vain! Mothering is a *"labor of love"* (1 Thessalonians 1:3).

This word "labor" is used to denote, "not so much the actual exertion of work, but the weariness that we experience, toil as in reducing strength, labor, weariness." I know that many times you feel weary. Sometimes you feel as though you have no strength left, but God's promise comes to encourage you, *"I will not forget your work and labor of love"* (Hebrews 6:10). You will receive your reward!

God will strengthen you each day, *"not the grim strength of gritting your teeth but the glory-strength God gives. It is strength that endures the unendurable and spills over into joy"* (Colossians 1:11, The Message). Isn't that wonderful?

3

Prayer:

"Father God, please help me to have an abounding attitude as I mother in my home—abounding in joy, fun, laughter, nurturing, sweetness, love, and wisdom. Amen."

Affirmation:

If I only do what is required of me, I am a slave. When I do more than is required, I am a free person.

Day 2

Good Workmanship

"Thus the two will be joined in a workmanlike fashion
and will never come apart"
(Exodus 28:28 Knox).

I am always amazed at the practicality of the Bible. God is interested in the practical details of our everyday lives. He gave explicit instructions on how to make everything for the tabernacle in the wilderness. He told Moses exactly how He wanted each piece of furniture and each piece of clothing to be made. God is a clothes designer and He planned the glorious garments for the High Priest to wear.

The High Priest also wore a breastplate and God gave precise instructions how the rings of the breastplate were to be tied to the rings of the ephod with blue cord. God is concerned about good workmanship. He showed Moses how to do it so it would never come apart. God wants things done properly. He does not want shoddy work.

I was brought up with the maxim, "If a job's worth doing, it's worth doing well." I am sure you did too. And now you are training your children the same way. We continue this training from generation to generation. It is important that we keep passing on this baton, because it is a biblical one.

Not only should we tackle each job to the very best of our ability, but if we start something, we should finish it. Sometimes we face obstacles in the things we start and we want to give up. When my father (who passed away at 91 years) faced a problem he would always say, **"A good man's never stuck!"** He always found a way to fix the problem and finish the job. His father passed on these words to him and they became part of his life. He passed them on to his children and grandchildren! Now my children and grandchildren are familiar with this statement and I often hear them quoting it.

God Himself shows us the example when He created the world. *"And God saw every thing that he had made and, behold, it was very good . . . thus the heavens and the earth were **finished**, and all the host of them"* (Genesis 1:31; 2:1).

What about King Solomon? 2 Chronicles 3:1 says, *"Then Solomon began to build the house of the Lord at Jerusalem in mount Moriah."* We then read in chapter 5:1, *"Thus all the work that Solomon made for the house of the Lord was **finished**."*

We also read about Zerubbabel in Zechariah 4:9, *"The hands of Zerubbabel have laid the foundation of this house;* **his hands shall also finish it.***"*

Jesus said, *"My food is to do the will of Him that sent me, and to* **finish His work***"* (John 4:34 and 17:4).

Paul had the same spirit when he confessed in Acts 20:24, *"None of these things move me, neither count I my life dear unto myself, so that I might* **finish my course** *with joy."* Also read 2 Timothy 4:7.

To see a job through to the end is a godly trait. Let's carry on God's example of good workmanship in our own lives and impart this godly character trait into the lives of our children and grandchildren.

Prayer:
"Father, please help me to reveal your character in my life by doing every job to the best of my ability. Help me to do everything in my home with good workmanship. And please help me to impart this habit to my children. Amen."

Affirmation:
Shoddy work does not belong in our family!

Day 3

The Joyful Life

"He makes the barren woman to keep house, and to be
a joyful mother of children. Praise ye the Lord"
(Psalm 113:9).

Flying to Washington State I had to connect with a bus to my destination. While waiting I engaged in conversation with the ticket master. As we talked about our children, I informed him that I was blessed to have over 30 grandchildren. He looked at me with bewilderment, and yet with sad, longing eyes.

"How do you do this in this world?" he asked. "My marriage is a challenge. We have a big home but we are a slave to it. My wife and I both work to keep up the payments. We could only afford two children and now we are trying to put them through college. Isn't this how everyone lives today?"

"Yes it is," I replied. "But it's not the way it's meant to be. You don't have to be a victim to the system. You don't have to follow what everyone else is doing. It is obvious you are miserable doing it."

A glint of truth began to dawn on his face. He was shocked into realizing that his life of bondage was not God's original intention.

"Whenever we go shopping, all my wife wants to do is to look at baby clothes," he continued. "She constantly talks about having a little grandchild. But of course, we can't have this enjoyment. We want them to get a degree, establish their career, and enjoy life before they settle down."

"I beg your pardon," I replied. "*Enjoy life?* To get married and have children is to enjoy life. To have grandchildren is to enjoy life. This is the real life. This is what life is all about."

"You've given me a lot to think about," he called out as I rushed to catch my bus.

Isn't it sad how society is sucked into a way of living that is far removed from God's original intention? Parents tell their children to make sure they enjoy their life before they get married. Young people want to do their own thing and "enjoy life" before settling down. They have been brainwashed into thinking that settling down and having children will not be enjoyable. On the other hand, God equates having children with joy. Motherhood is associated with joy as it tells us in Psalm 113:9.

Fatherhood is also associated with joy. Psalm 127:4-5 says, *"As arrows are in the hand of a mighty man; so are children of the youth. Happy is the man that has*

7

his quiver full of them." The word "happy" in this Scripture is a plural word and should read "Happy, happy!" or "How happy!" It is double happiness!

It is true that there are many unhappy mothers and fathers. I believe this is mostly because of mind attitude. Because society has brainwashed women to think that mothering is an inferior task and careerism is far more important, they feel miserable that they are bogged down with children who interfere with their life choices. They love their children, but they don't love motherhood! It is only when we embrace motherhood that we enter into the joy of it. As we do this, we begin to experience the fullness and anointing of motherhood which God intends us to walk in.

What groove are you walking in? The furrow of humanistic society or the furrow of God's original plan?

Prayer:
"Father, please save me from walking the wrong path. Lead me in the way you intended for me to live. Amen."

Affirmation:
God's way is the best way for me!

Day 4

God is Still with You

"When you pass through the waters, I will be with you; and through the rivers, they shall not overflow you. When you walk through the fire, you shall not be burned, nor shall the flame scorch you"
(Isaiah 43:2).

I never tire of reading the story of Joseph. I think of how he was so cruelly treated by his brothers and sold as a slave. As a young teenager, without warning, he was ripped away from his beloved father, his home, and his family which he loved. He was sold to Potiphar, the captain of Pharaoh's guard. Even though this must have been devastating to this young man, the Bible tells us in Genesis 39:3 that, *"the Lord with him, so that he prospered in all that he undertook."*

Because you are going through a difficult time, or because you suddenly land up in a terrible trauma does not mean that God is not with you. In fact, He may be more with you than you realize!

Joseph's situation became worse. Because of the false witness of Potiphar's wife, Joseph, although totally innocent, was thrown into prison. How much more could go wrong with his life? The amazing thing is that the Bible states in Genesis 39:21 Knox, ***"But the Lord was still with him."*** What an amazing Scripture. Even in prison, God was still with Joseph.

Do you think that your situation could not get any worse? Do you feel it is more than you can bear? I have wonderful news for you: God is **still** with you. He is not only with you when everything is going fine. He is with you in the worst situation. He will never leave you or forsake you. He knows what He is doing. He is working out things in your life far beyond what you can see.

There must have been many times when Joseph felt that he was forgotten, not only by his family and everyone else, but even by God. However, God was working. He was preparing Joseph for his destiny. He was working everything out for good, not only for his good, but for the blessing of his whole family—and the nation.

I love reading of the emotionally charged meeting when Joseph reunites with his brothers. He does not accuse them for their wicked deed. Instead, He acknowledges that God was in it all. Genesis 45:7-8 says, *"God sent me before you to preserve posterity for you in the earth, and to save your lives by a great deliverance. So it was not you who sent me here, but God.*" Joseph acknowledged that God was the instigator of all his hardships and years of loneliness and neglect.

Later, when Joseph was ruling Egypt and his father died, his brothers feared that he would bring retribution upon them for their wickedness. Instead, Joseph says, "*But as for you, you meant evil against me;* **but God meant it for good**, *in order to bring it about as it is this day, to save many people alive. Now therefore, do not be afraid: I will provide for you and your little ones. And he comforted them and spoke kindly to them*" (Genesis 50:20-21). Are you getting the message? God is working everything out for your good, and maybe for the good of many others.

Instead of groveling in your problems, thank God that He is still with you. I know it's hard to see while you are going through it. Nor could Joseph. But, do not look at what you can see. Trust in God and thank Him that He is with you.

I hear many women saying, "I'm going through deep waters, please help me!" or "I am going through the fire. It is so terrible." This is the wrong confession. Read again the wonderful promise in Isaiah 43:2. God says that when you go through the waters, "*I will be with you.*" He does not say that you will not go through the waters, but that He will be with you in them.

Change your confession. When you are going through the deep waters, cry out, "Thank you, Lord that you are with me. I thank you that I will not drown. I cannot drown because you are with me." When you are going through the fiery trial, change your confession to, "I will not be burned, because you are with me. Thank you for your mighty presence with me."

Will you believe God's precious promises? Even in the most difficult situation you can experience God's presence as you acknowledge that He is with you.

Prayer:

"Dear Lord, I cannot understand why I am going through this difficult situation, but I thank you that you are with me. I trust in your constant faithfulness to me. Amen."

Affirmation:

*God is **still** with me!*

Day 5

A Prickly Pear?

"As the lily among thorns, so is my love among the daughters"
(Song of Songs 2:2).

What a beautiful description of the bride of Christ. In the previous verse, Christ is described as the Lily of the Valleys and now she is described as the lily. What Christ is, we are to be in this world as the Scripture tells us in 1 John 4:17.

What do you imagine when you think of a lily? I think of . . .

Purity

I am sure your mind immediately thinks of the white Madonna lily with which we are so familiar and yet also grew in Israel. This beautiful flower has been an emblem of purity for thousands of years. This is the picture of the bride of Christ in this sinful world.

Humility

Our Bridegroom is called the Lily of the Valleys. Where He is we will be too. The lily does not grow on the heights but in the fertile valleys. The true believer is not high-minded and proud, but has a humble spirit.

Beauty

Jesus said that even King Solomon, the richest king in all his glory, could not compete with the beautiful lily.

Trust

Jesus exhorted us not to worry about what we will eat or wear and used the illustration of the lilies that do not toil or worry and yet God watches over them to protect and provide for them (Matthew 6: 25-34). Can we not trust Him too?

No Pricks

This is the rub. All around us there are thorny people who pierce us with their sharp and nasty words and who prick us with their actions. Maybe there are thorny people in your own home or family relationships. Their pricks can really hurt! How do you react? Can you continue to be a lily in these circumstances?

It is easy to be a lily among other lilies. The real test is to be a lily among the thorns!

How can you do this? Only by the power of the living Christ within you. It is the grace of God. It is His life in you. Jesus died and shed His blood to enable you to live as a lily among the thorns. When Jesus was pricked, He did not retaliate. When he was blasphemed and ridiculed he did not answer a word. Jesus who lives within you does not get prickly and upset. He does not get mad and shoot out thorns.

Stress and the pressures of life can also make you feel irritable and prickly, but Christ within you does not get stressed out, no matter how huge the problem.

Song of Songs 5:13 describes Christ, *"His lips like lilies, dropping sweet smelling myrrh."* Prickly words don't fall from his lips. His lips drop sweetness. What drops from your lips? Unkind or sweet words? How do you react to pressures or hurtful words in your home? Does everyone feel your prickles? It's not very nice being close to a prickly person, is it?

Can you allow the sweetness and purity of Christ to shine forth even when you are being pricked? Even when your husband is thorny?

Prayer:

"Oh Father, please take away the prickliness in my life. I often feel hurt and wounded, but please help me to react like the lily, to trust you instead of retaliating with sharp and unkind words. Amen."

Affirmation:

As He is, so am I in this world.

Sing This Song or Pray as a Prayer:

"Let the beauty of Jesus be seen in me,
All His wondrous compassion and purity,
Oh, Thou Spirit divine, all my nature refine
'Till the beauty of Jesus be seen in me."

Day 6

My Miracles?

"I will praise thee; for I am fearfully and wonderfully made: marvelous are thy works; and that my soul knoweth right well"
(Psalm 139:14).

You know that God is a miracle-working God. You believe it. You are in awe at how God stretched forth His mighty right arm to deliver the Israelites from the clutches of Egypt and how He brought them through the Red Sea on dry land. Yet, do you sometimes wonder why God doesn't do any personal miracles for you?

You don't have to wonder any longer! You already have miracles in your home. You are looking at them all day long! You are a miracle. Your husband is a miracle. Each one of your precious children is a miracle, created by God's miracle-working power.

David wrote under the inspiration of God when he stated that we are *"fearfully and wonderfully made."* He did not have access to ultra sound to see the intricate workings of the baby being formed in the secret place of the womb, but God wrote through him. The word translated *"wonderfully"* is the Hebrew word *palah*. It means "to distinguish." In other places in the Bible it is translated, "put a difference," "separated," and "set apart."

God reveals to us in this Scripture how He makes every new person in the world different, a special and unique person that has never lived before or will ever live again! Each one is distinguished from everyone else. Each one is set apart to be someone special and to fulfill a destiny that no one else can fulfill. "You are an unrepeatable miracle" as Rev. John Anderson shares. Amazing!

Look at each one of your children. They are special! An only-one-of-its-kind! See your children as miracles. Each one is irreplaceable. Each one has different gifts and callings and a different personality from you! Some children don't seem to "fit" your family style because God created them differently! Allow them to be the unique miracle God created them to be.

You can't be a stereotype parent. You have to call upon God for wisdom for each individual child. I am amazed at the different giftings in our children. They continually do things that are different to the bent that Colin or I have. This keeps life from getting boring! It enlarges our thinking and our coasts! It makes us realize that He is the Creator!

13

What about your husband? God created him exactly in the mold He planned for him! Why not stop trying to make him the way you want him to be. Instead, look at him as a God-planned miracle too? Take your hands off and let him be who God created him to be. He is God's creation, not yours.

Charles Spurgeon says, "We need not go to the ends of the earth for marvels, nor even across our own threshold; they abound in our own bodies." He also writes, "If we are marvelously wrought upon even before we are born, what shall we say of the Lord's dealings with us after we leave His secret workshop and He directs our pathways through the pilgrimage of life?"

It is interesting to note that David did not talk about his parents when he wrote of His creation. He ascribed it all to God. No matter whom the parents, every baby is a new miracle, created by God Himself. Even if a child is born of incest or prostitution, it does not change the fact that he or she is a special miracle, masterminded and fashioned by God for His glory and praise. S. D. Gordon says, "The new-born babe is a fresh act of God. He is the latest revelation of God's creative handiwork."

Surely we must exclaim again with the Psalmist, *"Know that the Lord, He is God; it is He who has made us, and not we ourselves"* (Psalm 100:3).

Prayer:

"Father God, I am sorry that I have taken my husband and children for granted. I acknowledge that they are miracles of your creation. Help me to always see them as miracles. Amen."

Affirmation:

My home is filled with miracles!

The Breathtaking Privilege:

"Every mother has the breathtaking privilege of sharing with God in the creation of new life. She helps bring into existence a soul that will endure for all eternity. Every mother also has the unique honor of nurturing and developing the bit of divine greatness in her child . . . a good mother can reach beyond the sanctuary of her home and help renew the face of earth."
~ James Keller

Day 7

A Happy Face

"The show of their countenance doth witness against them"
(Isaiah 3:9).

One morning as I walked with my daughters, Evangeline and Serene, I asked them, "How can we have a heavenly atmosphere in our homes?"

"Wear a happy face," Evangeline immediately answered.

I didn't expect that answer, but it was a good one. The face we wake up with will determine the atmosphere in our home for the day. Even if you feel depressed, it is important to put on a happy face, for your children and for your husband.

"But that's not being real," you answer.

I guess that depends on whether you prefer to give into your feelings or live by the power of Christ who lives within you! There are some who think that reality is living according to how you feel. Deception! True reality is found in the truth of Galatians 2:20 which is not living according to the dictates of my flesh or my emotions, but living the life of Christ who lives in me.

You will be amazed how your actions can change the way you feel. Perhaps you have been up all night with the baby. You feel tired. Put on a happy face anyway. Smile at your husband. Smile at each of your children. You'll begin to feel better right away. Yes, you will. Just try it.

Perhaps you are in a negative mood. Everything is going wrong and self-pity is taking over. It's already showing on your face! Stop. Look up to the Lord and thank Him for your blessings. Thank Him that He is near you and will never leave you or forsake you. Now show your happy face to your children. Your gloominess will soon leave.

A downcast face will lock you into tiredness or anxiety. A happy face will ignite a spark of joy in your heart. A miserable face will sink you into self-pity. Put on a smile, even if it is the last thing you feel like doing, and you will feel your heavy burden lift.

Proverbs 15:13 says, *"A merry heart makes a cheerful countenance."* The MLB says, *"A happy heart makes the face look sunny."*

Proverbs 15:15 TLB says, *"When a man is gloomy, everything seems to go wrong; when he is cheerful, everything seems right!"*

Proverbs 17:22 GNB says, *"Being cheerful keeps you healthy. It is slow death to be gloomy all the time."* Gloominess not only brings death to you, but to your whole family. It casts a shadow over your home.

In the same way you look to the Lord and are changed into His image (2 Corinthians 3:18), so your children look to you and are changed into your image. They copy your expression. If you are happy and smiling, you will have happy children. If you are miserable, you'll have whining children.

A smiling face and a positive attitude can become part of your life. Make it a habit. Show it by example to your children. Don't allow your children to get into moods, be grumpy, or pout! We never allowed this for one second in our children and they don't battle with any of these attitudes today.

Put on a happy face, and change the atmosphere of your home.

Prayer:
"Oh Lord, help me to remember that there is a higher truth than my feelings. It is the truth of your life in me, and this is the life I want to live. Thank you, Lord. Amen."

Affirmation:
Because I am smiling, my home is filled with smiling faces.

16

Day 8

All the Days of My Life

"One thing have I desired of the Lord, that will I seek after;
that I may dwell in the house of the Lord all the days of my life,
to behold the beauty of the Lord, and to inquire in his temple"
(Psalm 27:4).

David longed for the "house of the Lord." But David could not be in the house of the Lord continually, as much as he longed to. He was king of a nation. He had battles to fight; administration to attend to. Dear mother, we have the opportunity to live David's longing. Let me explain.

The house of the Lord is no longer one temple as it was in David's day. It is not even a church building where we attend on Sundays or Saturdays today. The house of the Lord speaks of His presence. God wants your home to be His house where His presence dwells; a place where you abide in Him and He abides in you. The house of the Lord is your kitchen where you prepare the meals; the house of the Lord is your dining table where you feed your family and make every meal a love affair; the house of the Lord is any room in the home where you are working or interacting with your children.

In your home you can behold the beauty of the Lord. As you abide in Him and look to Him, He will impart His grace to you in your time of need. He will show you that He is the "God who is Enough" for every challenge and every situation. He is with you in your home and will never leave you or forsake you. No, not even when everything seems overwhelming and you feel like tearing your hair out! You are still in the house of the Lord at that moment.

Instead of despairing about the situation, stop for a moment and realize that God is with you. He has promised that He will not fail you. Thank Him that He is with you and will never fail you.

David had to go to God's temple to inquire of the Lord. He faced battles, enemies, and challenges; He needed God's discernment, wisdom, and strength. You also need God's wisdom. You are desperate to know what to do. You cannot go on without His strength. Praise God, you don't have to get into your car and rush off to a church building. You are in the house of the Lord right now. You can inquire in His temple right now. He will give you His wisdom right now.

All you have to do is abide—that literally means to live in His presence. It means to acknowledge that Christ is living within you and that you are in

Him. You are inseparable. You are one. He is your life source. You can't live without Him (well, I can't anyway!).

Your strength wanes; you need His strength. Your wisdom is human; you need His divine wisdom. Your love runs out the door; you need His agape love. You are depressed and down in the dumps; His joy is greater than your feelings. You feel your life is worthless; you can only bear fruit to bless your family and touch other lives as you abide.

John 15:4-5 says, "*Abide in me, and I in you. As the branch cannot bear fruit of itself, except it abide in the vine; no more can ye, except ye abide in me. I am the vine, ye are the branches: He that abides in me, and I in him, the same brings forth much fruit; for without me can do nothing.*" See your home in a new light. It is the house of the Lord and you can live in it all the days of your life.

Prayer:

"Thank you, Lord, for showing me that my home is the house of the Lord. Help me to enjoy my home in a new way. Thank you that I don't have to visit the house of the Lord. I live in it! Amen."

Affirmation:

I am not a visitor, but a dweller in the house of the Lord.

One, Two, Three, Go!

*"Rise ye up, take your journey, and pass over the river Arnon: behold, I have given into thine hand Sihon the Amorite, king of Heshbon, and his land: **begin** to possess it, and contend with him in battle"*
(Deuteronomy 2:24).

Begin! What an important word.

Are you dreaming about doing something? Perhaps getting that bedroom cleaned up. Or catching up with the laundry. Maybe you have some great ideas about homeschooling you are planning to put into operation.

It's easy to dream about it, isn't it? It's a lot harder to do something. But there is a secret to accomplishing the thing you dream about doing. Simply begin! That's right. Start. Don't look at the whole job. It will put you off. Just start. It is amazing what happens when you begin. You'll be amazed how that room will soon be cleaned. You will be amazed at what you accomplish.

What about that habit you want to get rid of in your life? Begin tackling it. They say it takes three weeks to establish a new habit. Start today with a positive response to your bad habit. Keep it up for three weeks and you will win the victory.

What about that mountain that looms before you? That problem you feel you cannot face. Take a step to go after it. Everything happens with that first step! In fact, nothing happens without the first step! God told the children of Israel to **begin** to possess the land. They faced giants, fenced cities, high walls, and gates with bars, but they began . . . and they possessed. They didn't possess the land all at once. But they began. You will have to too. You have to go beyond your normal routine. You have to get out of your comfort zone.

In Exodus 23:29-30 God told His people, *"I will not drive them out from before thee in one year; lest the land become desolate, and the beast of the field multiply against thee. By **little and little** I will drive them out from before thee, until thou be increased and inherit the land."*

The big thing is to begin, then tackle the job, your vision, or the problem little by little. Little by little you will finish the task. Little by little you will overcome!

I think of my sister, Kate who was never able to have children. For years she prayed about adopting a little girl from China, but never had the finance to go ahead. She was 49 years old. The cut off was 50 years! I said, "Kate, you've just got to start!" So she did! With no money she started filling in the papers. As she forged ahead in faith, God provided along the way. Little by little she ended up fulfilling the payment of about $25,000 and getting her precious daughter, Promise from China. This miraculously happened with no opportunity of finance on her part.

I love the poem, *It Couldn't be Done* by Edgar Guest. This poem was required learning for our children. Some of the lines say . . .

> *Somebody scoffed: "Oh, you'll never do that;*
> *At least no one ever has done it!"*
> *But he took off his coat and he took off his hat,*
> *And the first thing we knew he'd **begun** it.*

Once you begin, don't stop until you conquer and win the victory. It will be hard work. You will face battles. God said, *"Begin to possess it, and contend with him in battle"* (Deuteronomy 2:24). The children of Israel did not win any victories without first having to fight a battle. It's part of possessing and overcoming.

The secret? The final victory starts with the verb, *begin*!

Prayer:

"Lord, please save me from procrastinating. Give me courage to take the first step to obey and do what you want me to do. Thank you, Lord. Amen."

Affirmation:

No more dreaming, I'm doing it today!

Day 10

My Resting Place

"Lay not wait, O wicked man, against the dwelling of the righteous;
spoil not his resting place"
(Proverbs 24:15).

What is the banner that flies over your home? Is it a banner of love? Unity? Joy? What about the banner of rest? Isn't it interesting that God calls the righteous home a *"resting place"*?

God wants your home to be a sanctuary of rest—a rest for you, a rest for your husband when he returns from the marketplace at the end of the day, and a place of rest for our children. He wants you to enjoy your *"resting place."* Sadly, we are often too busy running here and there that we don't have time to make our home a resting place. It takes time, thought, and prayer. And, it takes being there!

Recently my daughter, Evangeline, went to a homeschool Used Book Sale. On the way home her van broke down. What would she do? Her husband was in Sweden. My husband was away. I was taking my father to the airport to return to New Zealand. She thought of another family to call. They graciously came to her rescue and loaned her one of their cars to use until hers was fixed. But by the time she arrived home she was frazzled, especially after waiting in the hot car for about three hours with all the children and her newborn baby.

She eventually got the children settled for the night. She was settling down herself when one of the children starting crying with pain. She investigated and found that his private parts were severely swollen and red. He had an infection from tick bites and it looked serious. Her first thought was that she'd have to rush him to the hospital.

However, she took a moment to look to the Lord and open the Word of God. Her Bible opened to Isaiah 30:15, *"In returning and rest shall ye be saved; in quietness and confidence shall be your strength."* She knew this was the Lord speaking directly to her. She knew God wanted her to stay still and trust in Him. She didn't have to rush to the hospital. She had to stay home, rest, and trust God would heal her little boy.

She immediately made a mixture of Activated Charcoal, Echinacea, and Golden Seal, which she applied to the problem area—and she prayed. The next day she planned to go to another book sale but she knew she had to obey the Lord and stay home. The following day she'd planned to go to church in town,

21

but once again she stayed quietly at home. By applying the natural healers and staying quiet, her little boy was totally healed.

Dear mother, it is in quietness and stillness that God speaks to you and gives you wisdom. It is by the *"still waters"* you will hear His voice, giving you the answers you need to tackle the problems you face each day.

There's also a special time of each day that should be a resting time in each home. It's in the cool of the evening when the day's work is over. It's the time for rest and fellowship. It's the time when God wants to come and fellowship with us. Remember how God came to Adam and Eve to fellowship with them in the *"cool of the day"* (Genesis 3:8)?

Unfortunately, this is often the time when many mothers are still running hither and thither. They are out amongst the busy traffic, taking their children, or collecting their children from this and that. Satan robs them from their *"resting place."* This is the time when a mother should be in her home, preparing a meal for her husband and family, so they can all sit together around the table and rest and fellowship during *"the cool of the day."*

We as mothers have to make this happen. It is our responsibility. We either make it happen, or it will be robbed from us. God doesn't want our "resting place" spoiled. The word "spoil" in the Hebrew is *shaddad*, which means "to destroy, to rob." Are you letting the enemy use little things, subtle things, or even **good** things to rob you of your resting place? Do you feel the intensity in this Scripture when it says, *"**Spoil not** his resting place"*?

It's interesting that when God offers rest, there is often resistance. Look again at Isaiah 30:15, *"For thus saith the Lord God, the Holy One of Israel; In returning and rest shall ye be saved; in quietness and in confidence shall be your strength, **and ye would not**."*

Jeremiah 6:16 says, *"Thus saith the Lord, Stand ye in the ways, and see, and ask for the old paths, where is the good way, and walk therein, and ye shall find rest for your souls, but they said, **We will not walk therein**."*

Do you remember the heart cry of Jesus when he looked over Jerusalem and cried, *"O Jerusalem . . . how often would I have gathered thy children together, even as a hen gathereth her chickens under wings, **and ye would not**"* (Matthew 23:37)!

God calls you to come back into the heart of your home. He wants you to rest in your home. He wants your home to be the center of your life, where you live in quietness and confidence.

God is a God of rest. He wants to rest in your heart, but He also wants to rest in your home. In the Old Covenant, God chose Zion for His resting place. Psalm 132:13-14 says, *"For the Lord hath chosen Zion; he hath desired it for his habitation. This is my rest forever: here will I dwell; for I have desired it."*

Is your response, "No, Lord, I'd rather not, thanks all the same. Home is too boring for me. Plus, I've got to take my children to this lesson and that sport or they'll grow up deprived. And it's much easier to buy fast food on the way home than take time to cook a meal"?

Or, is it, "Yes, Lord, I will. I want to be planted in the heart of my home instead of rushing here and there. I want to make my home a resting place for you and my family"?

God shares His heart and desire for you in Isaiah 32:18, "*My people shall dwell . . . in quiet resting places.*" Is your home your resting place?

Prayer:

"Father, my house is full of tension. Please help me to make my home a resting place. Show me the things I am doing that spoil the rest in our home. Give me strength and courage to change and eliminate these things from my lifestyle. Amen."

Affirmation:

I say "Yes" to God's offer of rest.

The Secret of Peace:

"In acceptance lieth peace,
O my heart be still;
Let thy restless worries cease
And accept His will.
Though this test be not thy choice,
It is His—therefore rejoice."
~ Hannah Hurnard

Day 11

Above Only

Part 1

*"And the Lord shall make thee the head, and not the tail; and Thou shalt be **above only**, and thou shalt not be beneath; if thou hearken unto the commandments of the Lord thy God, which I command thee this day, to observe and to do them"*
(Deuteronomy 28:13).

Where do you live? Groaning under your circumstances? Or, are you on top, looking down on them from a place of victory? It's so easy to go under, isn't it? It doesn't take any effort at all. It takes a lot more effort to stay on top. But you can get into the habit of doing it. All you have to do is to change your current thought habits and switch gear into a new mindset.

When Peter wrote to the new believers who were scattered throughout the country that is called Turkey today, he encouraged them to, *"gird up the loins of your mind"* (1 Peter 1:13). The Modern Language Bible translates it well, *"Brace up your minds for action, and be alert."* These believers understood what he was talking about. In those days, they wore long flowing robes. If they wanted to run or exercise, they had to pull up their robes and secure them so they would not be hindered in their action.

This is what you have to do with your mind. When you feel like you are coming under your circumstances, gird up your mind. Capture your negative thoughts and oust them from you. Instead of agonizing over your problems, look down upon them from God's vantage point. Remember where God has placed you in the spirit realm. You have been lifted up to sit with Christ Jesus in the heavenly spheres (Ephesians 2:6). See yourself there, looking down upon your problems.

Perhaps you feel overwhelmed in your home. Everything is in a mess. See yourself looking down upon it. From that vantage point, you'll begin to see solutions to the problem. God has a practical answer for every difficulty or frustration you face in your home, but you will never see the way out while you are complaining and crying in the dust. You've got to look down from your position in Christ. As you do this, you'll see things in their true perspective and the revelation for victory will come!

God's Word says you will be *"above only"* and *"not be beneath."* Wait a minute. There is a prerequisite. This promise is only to those who fully obey the commandments of the Lord. As you walk in obedience to the Lord, you can claim this promise.

Choose where you want to be today. Don't let Satan take your mind captive. He laughs when you are in a miserable state. He wants you to feel like a failure. Instead, *"tear down reasonings and every proud barrier that is raised up against the knowledge of God and lead every thought into subjection to Christ"* (2 Corinthians 10:5 MLB).

God's plan for you today is to be above only! Be there!

Prayer:

"Father, I thank you for the amazing revelation, that because I am in you, I have been raised up to sit with you in the heavenly realm. This is beyond my natural thinking, but it is the truth. Help me to believe and live in this truth. Help me to see my problems from my position of sitting with you in heavenly places. Amen."

Affirmation:

I choose to live where Christ has placed me.

Day 12

Above Only

Part 2

*"Blessed **above women** shall Jael the wife of Heber the Kenite be,
blessed shall she be **above women** in the tent"*
(Judges 5:24).

Have you ever read the story of Jael in Judges chapters 4 and 5? If not, it's worth reading. But, I must warn you. It is rather gory. Perhaps I better tell you what she did in case you don't get time to read the whole story today.

When Sisera, captain of the king of the Canaanites, was fleeing from the victorious Israelites, he ran to the tent (home) of Jael. She brought him into her tent, gave him food, and let him sleep. However, while he was asleep, she took a hammer and a sharp tent peg, quietly crept up to him, and nailed the peg through his temples! At her feet he lay dead!

I wonder why Jael was praised so profusely for such a bloodthirsty deed. A number of translations say, *"**Most blessed** of women is Jael . . ."*

I believe she was praised because she took authority over the enemy! It must have been a very scary thing for her as a woman. She was obviously all alone. But, she knew that there would never be peace in their land while this man lived! She had to take action. In doing so, she became blessed above all other women in their homes.

Dear mother, you have enemies that surreptitiously creep into your home. You have enemies that seek to undermine your marriage. You have enemies around you in society that want to steal your children from their divine purpose on this earth. Don't let them linger around. Take authority over them in the power of the name of Jesus Christ. If you are walking in obedience to the Lord and His word, you have this authority in His name.

Jesus said to His disciples in Luke 10:19, *"Behold, I give unto you power . . . over all the power of the enemy."*

If you want victory in your home, you as the mother must live in the victory. You must live above, and not beneath. This is the overcoming life. The eternal crowns and rewards are promised to the overcomers. Now, if there is nothing in your life to overcome, how can you be an overcomer? Life is full of challenges, difficulties, and problems. You either live under them or above them!

At one time my son was involved in a huge mind-blowing project, thwarted with constant problems. Talking to him one day, I comfortingly asked, "How are you getting on with all your problems?"

"I don't have problems," he replied, "only challenges!" Every new problem is a challenge to overcome.

Will you live above today?

Prayer:

"Lord, I know that in you, I am "above" in all circumstances. Help me to remember this. Thank you for the victory that you give me. Help me to be an overcomer today in the power of the name of Jesus. Amen."

Affirmation:

I am pounding Jael's tent peg through the enemies of my mind and home!

Day 13

Above Only

Part 3

*"Who can find a virtuous woman, for her price is far **above** rubies"*
(Proverbs 31:10).

When you walk in victory and authority in your home, you are above rubies (higher than precious gems) and above all other women in the home.

Deuteronomy 28:13 NIV says, *"If you pay attention to the commands of the Lord . . . and carefully follow them, you will always be at the top, and never at the bottom."* Don't you like that statement? *"Always at the top, and never at the bottom!"* Keep repeating this statement throughout this week and you'll be amazed at the changes that will happen.

One of the greatest secrets to live above your daily problems is your confession. What you speak has power to affect your life, your circumstances and the lives of your children in your home. Make sure your confession is positive.

Here are some affirmations for you to speak out loud today . . . and every day!

I am ABOVE grumbling, complaining and self-pity.

I am ABOVE listening to negative thoughts about my husband and my marriage. I am bound by covenant.

I am ABOVE the lure of being squeezed into the mold of this world's system.

I am ABOVE being intimidated by the antagonists of God's truth. I am on a narrow road that leads to life.

I am ABOVE the fallacy that I am "just a housewife." I am in the perfect will of God as I train my children to affect the course of this nation.

I am ABOVE the temptation to leave my divine career of motherhood for a lesser career that only brings earthly reward.

I am ABOVE the deceiving humanistic philosophies that infiltrate the media and society around me.

I am ABOVE the trials and frustrations that encompass me about.

I am ABOVE the tales and petty talk of the gossipers.

I am ABOVE self-preoccupation. I give room in my heart and mind for the needs of others.

I am ABOVE the pressure to "keep up with the Joneses." I don't have to have everything everyone else has.

Don't forget to speak these affirmations out loud. It is not enough to think them in your mind.

Prayer:

"Lord, help me today to speak positive words. Help me to speak only words of victory. Amen."

Affirmation:

"Always at the top, and never at the bottom!"

A Poem for You and Your Children:

The following is a little poem I taught to our children when they were young and they still quote it today. You may like to teach it to your children, too.

Two Little Men

Two little men stood looking at a hill,
One was named, *Can't* and one was named, *Will*.
Can't said, "I never in the world can climb this hill,"
So there he is at the bottom of it still!
Will said, "I'll get to the top because I will."
Two little men are living by the hill,
At the bottom is *Can't*, at the top is *Will*!

Day 14

Ask the Right Questions

"You should keep asking each other, 'What is the Lord's answer?'
or 'What is the Lord saying?'"
(Jeremiah 23:35 NLT).

Recently, a dear friend came to stay with us for a couple of weeks. On her arrival, she caught up with all the family news. Serene told her of her recent miscarriage at three months pregnant and she responded with, "And what did you learn through it, Serene?" Serene told me later that Sally's question really provoked her to think more about what she learned from this experience.

It was a growth question. Too often we ask negative questions of ourselves and even of others. "Why should I have to go through this experience?" "Why has this happened to me?" "What have I done to deserve this?" "Why do I have to live in this cramped house, I deserve a better one?" These are negative questions that come from a root of self-pity or a misunderstanding of the nature of our God.

When the children of Israel came into the wilderness, God miraculously and daily provided them with manna. But they soon got tired of it and longed for the food they ate in Egypt. Numbers 11 tells us that they wept tears as they cried out, *"Who will give us flesh to eat?"* God was displeased with their complaining question. He said He would answer their cry and send them flesh, not just for one day, but for a whole month, so much that it would come out their nostrils! And He sent judgment upon them at the same time. Complaining displeases God because it undermines His faithfulness.

Don't you think it would be a good idea to get into the habit of changing our questions to a positive level? Instead we could ask, "Lord, what are you trying to show me in this situation?" "In what way do you want to change me and enlarge my understanding of you?" Not one of us can avoid going through difficult times in our lives. However, if we sulk and groan in these circumstances, we'll never grow.

We mature through adversity. Maybe God wants to expose something in our lives that is not pleasing to Him. Maybe He is stirring up our nest in order to lead us in a different direction. This is often the only way God can get us to change. Maybe we have been trusting in our own abilities and possessions and this situation will cause us to seek His face and learn to trust Him.

It is not easy to go through hard times, but it is always for our good. David wrote Psalm 4 while he was going through one of the most heart-wrenching times of his life. His very own son, Absalom, had risen up against him and was seeking to take his crown and kingdom from him. I am sure there could be nothing more grieving than to be betrayed by your own son. But, as he was fleeing for his life from Absalom, he wrote the words, *"Thou hast enlarged me when I was in distress"* (Psalm 4:1). Also read Psalm 18:19; 31:8 and 118:5.

The Psalmist also confesses in Psalm 119:67, 71 and 75, *"Before I was afflicted I went astray: but now have I kept thy word." "It is good for me that I have been afflicted." "Thou in thy faithfulness hast afflicted me."*

Many years ago, I remember reading in one of Watchman Nee's books about a woman who noticed another lady crying profusely. She went up to her and instead of the usual, "What's the matter, dear?" she asked her, "Who are you crying for?" Was she crying for herself or were her tears for another? Many times our questions lead to self-pity, rather than growth. Often we use all our tears upon ourselves so that we have no emotions left to pour out in intercession and care for others.

May God help us to change our questions to those that will help bring us into growth, rather than leave us in the rut, or the pit of despair. God loves us too much to leave us where we are. He is not content with letting us stay the same. He wants to lead us on. He wants to change us into the likeness of Christ, from one degree of glory to another. If God did not allow difficulties to come to our lives, we'd stagnate instead of grow.

Let's ask this question continually, "Lord, what are you saying to me? I am listening as I read your precious Word. I want to hear you speak into my heart. What are you telling me through these circumstances I am going through?"

Prayer:

"Father, I want to take my eyes off myself and how things affect me. Please, lift up my eyes to see what you are doing in my life. I know your ways are higher than my ways and your thoughts are higher than my thoughts. I don't want to stay in the ditch of despair. I don't want to crouch in a complaining corner. I want to lift up my eyes, my soul, and my hands and praise you in the midst of my affliction. Thank you, Lord. Amen."

Affirmation:

"But to act, that each to-morrow find us farther than today."
~ Henry Wadsworth Longfellow

Day 15

Are You Kind?

*"Now the rest of the acts of Josiah, **and his goodness (kindnesses)**, according to that which is written in the law of the Lord, and his deeds, first and last, behold, they are written in the book of the kings of Israel and Judah"*
(2 Chronicles 35:26-27 and 2 Chronicles 32:32).

What a wonderful obituary over the life of Josiah. Josiah was a mighty king of Judah. He was a radical reformist. He spearheaded the greatest purging revival against evil in the land of Judah. He instigated the best Passover feast that was ever held from the time of Samuel. But the first thing the inspired Word of God records over his life is his *"kindnesses."* This attribute meant more to God than all his mighty acts.

The Hebrew word is *chesed*, one of the most beautiful words in the Old Testament. It means, "kindness, grace, mercy, beauty, and unfailing love." It is the same word that is used of God's lovingkindnesses. It also involves forgiveness and is the closest word to *charis*, the New Testament word for grace.

Each Friday evening that we are home, we love to celebrate a Shabbat meal and invite different friends and family to enjoy this precious time with us. At this meal, the husband reads Proverbs 31 and blesses his wife and children. At one Shabbat meal, I was touched by the testimony of one couple. The husband held his wife's hand and shared beautiful things about her, but the preeminent attribute he declared over her life was her kindness. "She is so very kind," he exclaimed. "She is so kind to me, the children, and even to her animals." What a beautiful testimony. Can we allow our kind and loving God to pour out His kindnesses through us?

Our God is not only kind, but abundantly kind. God's kindness (*chesed*) is always recorded with an adjective.

Exodus 34:6, *"**Abundant** in kindness."*

Nehemiah 9:17, *"Thou art a God, ready to pardon, gracious and merciful, slow to anger and of **great** kindness."*

Psalm 31:21, *"Blessed be the Lord: for he hath showed me his **marvelous** kindness."* Read also Psalm 17:7.

Psalm 36:7, *"How **excellent** is thy lovingkindness, O God."*

Psalm 69:16, *"Thy lovingkindness is **good**."*

Psalm 119:76, *"Let, I pray thee, thy **merciful** kindness be for my comfort."*

Isaiah 54:8, *"With **everlasting** kindness will I have mercy on thee, saith the Lord thy Redeemer."*

Seven adjectives!

It is not enough to be kind. It is not enough to do kind things. We must also speak kind words. The testimony of the *Above Rubies* woman in Proverbs 31:26 says, *"She opens her mouth with wisdom; and in her tongue is the **law of kindness**."* The Hebrew word used here is also *chesed*. It is not enough to speak kind words sometimes, nor is it enough to speak kindly to people at church on Sunday. We should speak kind words to those who are closest to us—our husband and children. It is a law in the depths of our being and should pour from our lips, even when people speak unkindly to us.

Prayer:

"Dear kind and loving God, I need to be more kind. I long to be saturated in your kindness. Please fill me with your lovingkindess so that I can pour it out to others. Anoint me to speak kind words, first to those in my home, and then to those around me. Amen."

Affirmation:

I don't want to be remembered for my great deeds, but for my kindnesses.

Day 16

Goodies and Baddies

*"The wedding is ready . . . go ye therefore into the highways, and as many
as ye shall find, bid to the marriage. So those servants went out into the
highways, and gathered together all as many as they found, **both bad
and good:** and the wedding was furnished with guests"*
(Matthew 22:8-10). Read the whole story of the
Wedding Banquet in Matthew 22:1-14.

The heavenly kingdom is going to be filled with not only good people, but
millions of bad people. Yes, that's right. God invites all the bad people, as many
as will come. What do you think of that? There's only one condition. They have
to wear the wedding garment. This speaks of the robe of righteousness which
we receive when our sins are cleansed and forgiven through the precious out-
poured blood of Jesus.

The guests were all seated at the banquet. The king arrived. He noticed
one guest who did not have on a wedding garment. The Bible does not tell
us whether this guest was one of the "goodies" or one of the "baddies," but I
have a feeling it was one of the "goodies." I think the baddies would have felt
so guilty and conspicuous without a wedding garment that they would have
made sure they had one. The king also referred to this man as his "friend."
Maybe he knew him. But perhaps this good guy thought he didn't need one.
He was a good person. He lived a good life and helped people whenever he
saw a need. What did he need to be covered for?

But, his good works were not enough. No matter who we are, good or bad,
we must have a wedding garment. We have to be cleansed by the blood of
Jesus. We need a robe of righteousness which only Christ can give us. We can't
make this robe ourselves. It is a gift from God.

Isaiah 64:6 says, *"But we are all as an unclean thing, and all our righteousnesses are as filthy rags . . ."* David says in Psalm 14:3, *"They are all gone aside, they
are all together become filthy: there is none that doeth good, no, not one."* Even our
piousness and all our "righteousnesses" are filthy. Actually, the word literally
means "stinking!"

What happened to this "good" person? When the king asked how he was
there without a wedding garment, he was speechless! There'll be no excuse
good enough if we don't have a garment. The king then told his servant to,

34

"Bind him hand and foot, and take him away, and cast him into outer darkness; there shall be weeping and gnashing of teeth."

At our *Above Rubies* retreats we like to take time on the last day for testimonies. This is always a very precious time and we make sure the tissue box is handy! I am amazed as I hear the testimonies of some of the mothers. They look as though they are one of the "goodies"—happy, home-making, child-loving mothers. But when they open their mouth and share the degradation from where God has delivered them, I stand in awe at the power of God. There is no sin that is too hard for God to forgive. There is no pit into which we fall that God cannot deliver us. He delights in redeeming the baddies and making them into new creations. He delights to wash them with His blood and cover them with His robe of righteousness.

Maybe you have never been a baddie. You are one of the goodies. You need the robe just as much. You'll never get into the Marriage Supper of the Lamb without your wedding garment, without repenting of all your "fleshly good works" and being covered with the blood of Jesus.

We must also lead our children to salvation. They can be brought up in a Christian home. They can grow up to be good people, but if they do not acknowledge their sinfulness and receive Christ as their Savior, they will not receive a wedding garment. To have Christian parents is not enough. To go to church is not enough. To be homeschooled is not enough. They must receive Christ's offer of salvation, when he died on the cross to pay the penalty for their sins.

1 John 1:7-9 says, *"The blood of Jesus Christ His Son cleanses us from all sin. If we say that we have no sin, we deceive ourselves, and the truth is not in us. If we confess our sins, he is faithful and just to forgive us our sins, and to cleanse us from all unrighteousness."*

May we, and each one of our children, receive the wedding garment.

Prayer:

"Oh God, I confess my sin before you. I confess that I have tried to run my own life. I've thought I could do it better than you. Lord, I confess my rebellion and disobedience. I turn to you and ask you to cleanse me with your precious blood. Make me your child and one of your family. Amen."

Affirmation:

"What can wash away my sin?
  Nothing but the blood of Jesus!
What can make me whole again?
  Nothing but the blood of Jesus!"

Day 17

Queen of Your Home

Part 1 – Governing the Home

"The woman, the mistress of the house"
(1 Kings 17:17).

Dear homemaker, how do you picture yourself in your home? Trapped? Imprisoned? Downgraded? Bored? Frustrated? Or, are you reigning as Queen of your home?

God intends you to reign as queen. The Old Testament calls you "the mistress of the house." The Hebrew word for "mistress" is *baalah* which is simply the feminine word for *baal*. It means "to be master, to have dominion over."

There is another word that is also used for "mistress" in the Old Testament. It is the Hebrew word *ghereth*. Once again, it is the feminine word of master, *gbiyr* and means "to be strong, valiant, to prevail."

It is not only men who want to have dominion. There is something in a woman that wants to have dominion also. Immediately after God told Adam and Eve to, "*Be fruitful, and multiply, and replenish the earth,*" He then said to them, "*Subdue it, and have dominion . . .*" These words were not only spoken to the man, but to the woman.

Now just a minute, I am not leading you down a path of deception. I am not saying you should rule your husband. Let's get things straight. We are privileged to submit to our husband's leadership, authority, and protection. However, under his covering and protection, God has given us a sphere of rulership—a realm where we are to rule and reign! What is this domain? It is our home.

God wants you to be the "mistress," governing over the domestic affairs of your home. Your home is the center of your life. It is a place of challenge, creativity, and celebration. You rule over your kitchen, making sure that your husband and family are daily nurtured with nutritious life-giving meals. You preside over the education of your children. You administrate the cleaning of your home. You direct the ideas, the projects, and the plans that you and your children are currently working on.

You practice hospitality, planning when you will invite each particular family or lonely person to come and eat at your table. You think about what you will feed them and how you can make them feel special. You work on assignments with your children in order to reach out to the poor and needy. You are constantly making your home a creative, interesting, and sacred place to live in.

You plan, plant, weed, and harvest your garden to feed your family and beautify your home. And of course you are full-time nurturing, loving, and encouraging your husband and children. Your life is FULL! There is so much to reign over. You never have enough time to fulfill all your great visions. Of course, as queen of your home, you are not doing everything yourself, but training your children in all these areas, too.

Yet, there are many who are bored with their home. They have not yet seen the vision that their home is their greatest sphere of influence for God. They do not have the vision for raising children for God. With no vision for hospitality and so little to rule over, they are unfulfilled and have to find their place of dominion elsewhere.

Unfortunately, they move out of the sphere where God wants them to govern. They come out from their husband's protection and become vulnerable to other men instead of their own husband. The result is an epidemic of divorce and breakdown of marriage, even in the Christian world.

Let's find fulfillment in the great opportunity God has given to us in our home.

Prayer:

"Oh God, I thank you for your divine plan for my life. Thank you for giving me the privilege of my home where I can live and work for you, nurturing and training my children, and making it a safe and sacred place for my husband. I thank you, Lord, that in my home I can find my greatest fulfillment. Amen."

Affirmation:

I am a fulfilled and liberated home-maker.

More Scriptures about the "Mistress" of the Home.

Genesis 16:8-9; 2 Kings 5:3; Psalm 123:2 and Isaiah 24:2.

Day 18

Queen of Your Home

Part 2 – Watching the Home

"I will therefore that the younger women marry, bear children, guide the house, give none occasion to the adversary to speak reproachfully"
(1 Timothy 5:14).

The New Testament also gives us the same understanding that we are to be the rulers of our homes. The phrase, *"guide the house"* is the Greek word *oikodespoteo*. It is a combination of two words:

oikos—home, household, family

despotace—master, ruler

Here we have the same meaning again, that God has given to women the charge, **not to manage their husband's lives, but to manage their own households.** We have the responsibility from God to keep our homes running smoothly.

We have the testimony of the woman in Proverbs 31:27, *"She looks well to the ways of her household, and eats not the bread of idleness."* The Hebrew word for *"looks well"* is *tsaphah* and it has two meanings.

1) To observe, to keep watch

Dear mother, don't look at all the other things that you could be doing outside your home. Instead, look to the things that need to be taken care of in your home today. There's a lot to do. Is the laundry up-to-date? Are the dishes washed? Is your home running smoothly? Are you watching over the minds and hearts of your children? Are you watching in prayer?

2) To lean forward, to peer into the distance

The diligent mother not only watches over the daily affairs of her home, but also looks ahead. She has stores of water and food in case of an emergency.

More than that, she looks into the future and makes decisions, based not only on the present, but how they will affect the future of her children. She also knows that mothering is not just for today but for the years ahead and the generations to follow. This mother knows that she is training children for God's divine purposes. Because she sees the bigger picture, the constant little things that go wrong from day to day do not frustrate her. She knows that pouring her heart into her home and teaching and training her children will have national and eternal consequences.

I love the words of Rev. T. De Witt Talmage, "Thank God, O woman, for the quietude of your home, and that you are queen in it. Men come at eventide to the home; but all day long you are there, beautifying it, sanctifying it, adorning it and blessing it. Better be there than wear a queen's coronet. Better be there than carry the purse of a princess. It may be a very humble home. There may be no carpet on the floor. There may be no pictures on the wall. There may be no silks in the wardrobe; but, by your faith in God, and your cheerful demeanor, you may garniture that place with more splendor than the upholsterer's hand ever kindled."

Your home is not a prison to restrict your life. It is a place where God can use you to influence many lives for Him, firstly your children, and multitudes of others who will come into your home over the years. My greatest delight is to bring people into our home, feed them at our table and by God's grace, show them His love and lead them closer to God.

I also love the words my daughter, Pearl, wrote about her grandmother, my mother. "It was in her kitchen that she welcomed friends and those who were lonely. An herb tea made in a pottery teapot and 'something nourishing to eat' were the items on her menu during visiting hours, though there never seemed to be a closing time. But, it wasn't just for the homemade food they came. It was the listening ear she offered and the well-chosen words of counsel. Her kitchen was not only a place to feed the hungry. It was a psychiatry office with a stool for a couch."

Dream about the wonderful things that can happen in your home.

Prayer:

"Father, please help me to make my home a beautiful place for you to dwell and a peaceful home for my family to live in. Show me how I can serve you and serve people in my home, rather than rushing out to meetings and leaving my children. Amen."

Affirmation:

My home is an exciting place to live. It is an exciting place to serve God. It is the best place to fulfill all my visions and dreams.

Day 19

Queen of Your Home

Part 3 – Working at Home

*"Older women likewise are to be reverent in their behavior, not malicious gossips, nor enslaved to much wine, teaching what is good, that they may encourage the young women to love their husbands, to love their children, to be sensible, pure, **workers at home**, kind, being subject to their own husbands, that the word of God may not be dishonored"*
(Titus 2:3-5 NASB).

I believe in working women. God believes in working women. However, God has ordained the place where they are to work. It is in the home. Before God created the woman He prepared a garden home ready for her. He designed this place for her to work. It is perfect for creativity. It is most suited for optimum results. It is the most protected environment. It is where God intended children to be raised. It is where you will accomplish the most for God. In the heart of your home you are in the perfect will of God.

When asked, "Do you go to work?" your immediate reply should be, "Yes, of course!"

"Where do you go to work?" the question continues.

"In the best place, my home," you reply.

Accept your home as the place where God has chosen for you to work. And remember it is a place to work! When you get up, get dressed, ready to tackle the day's work. Don't loaf around in your dressing gown, drinking cups of coffee when an important work awaits you.

Motherhood is not an insignificant task. You have the most important and influential work in the nation as you build a strong, stable home and raise children who will determine the future of the nation and even the world!

This work is taxing. This work takes all your physical and emotional strength. This work takes prayer. And contrary to humanistic propaganda, building a home and raising a family for God takes brainpower. You can't do it effectively part time. You can't do it lolling around. You have to get to work!

There are two early manuscripts from which the Bible is translated. Regarding today's Scripture, some translate the phrase *"keepers at home"* as *oikouros*. This is a combination of two words:

oikos—home and *ouros*—guard = guardian of the home

40

Other translations use the word, *oikourogo* which is also a combination of two words:

oikos—home and *ergon*—work = worker at home

Dear lovely mother, don't complain about all you have to do. Complaining drains your energy. Realize it is all part of your great job assignment. Roll up your sleeves, go to work and do it. God is your employer and He has given you your home in which to accomplish this great work. Make your home a lovely environment in which to work. Make it a safe, secure, stable, serene, sound, and sanctified place in which to raise your children.

Don't approach your work with resignation and negativity. Do it with joy. It's great fun to confess, "I love to work." God designed for us to work. He introduced it before the fall of man. It is for our blessing. And hard work won't kill you. You'll feel tired, but you'll sleep well! In fact, the harder your work, the better you'll sleep. Work with a good attitude—willingly, joyfully, fervently, faithfully, without grumbling, and do everything as unto the Lord.

Prayer:

"Oh God, I thank you for giving me my home in which to work and serve you. Thank you that this is the place you have chosen for me to raise our children. Help me to work diligently as I train them for you and make my home a clean, wholesome environment to fulfill my great commission. Amen."

Affirmation:

I am a working woman in my home. I will be the best employee for my heavenly employer.

Day 20

The Nurturing Anointing

"In all their affliction He was afflicted, and the angel of His presence saved them: in His love and in His pity He redeemed them; and He bare them, and carried them all the days of old"
(Isaiah 63:9).

I love the words of Serene's song, *El Shaddai*, from the album, *Peace All Over Me*.

As I hold this baby in my arms
I'm like a picture of you,
To nurture with your love
Is what you made me to do.

These words, *"To nurture with your love is what you made me to do"* should ring in the ears and hearts of all women. This is our highest destiny. This is what we were created and destined to do. This is the anointing God wants us to live in. It is an expression of who God is. Read Deuteronomy 1:31; 32:10-12 and Isaiah 46:3-4.

"To nurture." What beautiful words! The world is crying out for nurture. Children are crying to be nurtured. There are millions of adults across the world who need nurturing. They did not receive nurture when they were young and their lives are now bereft.

This "nurturing anointing" is not only relegated to mothers with children. It is God's intention for all women. If we were to ask who the greatest mother of this last century was, there would be a unanimous reply, Mother Theresa. Was she married? No. Did she bear her own children? No. But, she was a great nurturer. She fed the poor. She loved the unlovely. She poured out her life to the needy. She sacrificed her own goals to bless others.

The world waits to feel the anointing of God's nurturing heart. And it starts with us. It starts in our homes. It starts with pouring out our lives to nurture our own children and then flowing over to meet the needs of the needy around us.

Nurturing is not something that we do at certain times of the day. Nurturing is a lifestyle. It should constantly flow from us, to all we speak to and all we meet. Nurturing our children is a full-time job. We don't clock in our time and clock out again at a certain hour. Instead, we lay down our lives to pour out God's nurturing love.

The dictionary tells us that "nurture" means "that which nourishes such as food and that which promotes growth—education, training, and instruction."

Nurturing touches the whole person—body, soul, and spirit. We are to nurture our children's physical bodies with life-giving food. Remember that life-giving food is not refined, packaged, sugar-filled foodless food. It is not a diet from the fast food chains. It is enzyme-packed food that nourishes healthy bodies for the future.

What about the soul? Preparing food takes time, but it takes more effort to nurture the soul and the spirit. It is a full-time job. We nurture the soul by . . .

Encouragement

Encouragement is a powerful tool. It makes the soul fat and flourishing. Perhaps you were not encouraged as a child. You may still feel the loss of that in your life today, but don't deprive your children. Ask God, who is the God of consolation and encouragement, to pour His encouragement into you so you can encourage your children and feed their souls.

Training, Instruction, and Correction

This is the meaning of the word that is used in Ephesians 6:4 where it admonishes fathers, "*Do not provoke your children to wrath, but bring them up in the training and admonition of the Lord.*" We train and discipline our children because we love them and want them to be sharpened and polished ready for the Master's use. A child that is left to his own devices is not a nurtured child. It is sad to see children who are out of control and who have no boundaries. They may get what they want by whining and persistence but they grow up empty and dry in their souls.

In Jeremiah 31, God proclaims all the wonderful promises to His people Israel when they return to their land. One of them is in verse 12, "*their soul shall be as a watered garden.*" Wouldn't it be wonderful if all our children could testify to this blessing because of our faithful nurturing and watching over their souls?

And, of course, we nurture the spirit by feeding and nourishing our children in the ways and words of the Lord. I am sure that your longing is the same as mine that they will be "*nourished up in the words of faith and of good doctrine.*" (1 Timothy 4:6).

May the anointing of God's nurturing heart be poured upon you today—to minister to your own precious children and the hurting and needy around you.

Prayer:

"Father, please release your nurturing heart upon me, in me, and through me. I long to live in this anointing. Nurture me, Lord, as I wait on you, so I can nurture my family. I want to be a nurturer every moment of the day. Amen."

Affirmation:

I am created to be a nurturer.

El Shaddai

To listen to Serene and Pearl sing El Shaddai, go to: http://aboverubies.org/ElShaddai

Day 21

Town or Country

"If you will diligently obey the Lord your God, being careful to do all His commandments . . . Blessed shall you be in the city, and blessed shall you be in the country. Blessed shall be the offspring of your body . . ."
(Deuteronomy 28:1-4 NASB).

Some people love to live in the city. Some love the country. There are others who live in the city but who long to move to the country. They think that this will be a better life for their children. That may be so, but God has promised, if we are obedient to His commandments, to bless us whether we live in the town or the country.

If you are hankering to live in the country, and yet there is no way for you to do this, stop pestering your husband and be content. The requirement for God's blessing upon you and your family is not where you live, but whether you are obeying God's Word.

We now live in the country. I love it. I prefer it to the city. But through all the years of raising our children we lived in the city. They were wonderful years and God blessed us. I remember when we moved from New Zealand to Australia, not just to a new country, but to the playground of Australia, Surfer's Paradise. Our home looked out on the casino! Help! How do you raise teenagers in this environment?

Because this is where God sent us to serve Him, He blessed us and our children. Instead of being on the defensive, they were on the offensive for God. All the children, teens and younger, preached every weekend in the open air mall in Surfer's Paradise. They helped us grow the church. They are all loving and serving the Lord today.

When we moved to America, we lived in an apartment complex. By this time, only Pearl and Serene were still at home, the others all married. We squashed ourselves, and the *Above Rubies* office, into the apartment and opened our doors in hospitality, filling it with people and gathering them around our table for meals. We now live in a bigger home, but we had wonderful times in that dingy apartment.

By the way, here is a secret for getting a bigger home. Fill the one you have. Fill it with children. Fill it with people as you reach out in hospitality. When God sees you filling up the home you have, He will open doors for you to get a bigger one!

Some folks think that it is too difficult to have children in the city. However, the next words God speaks after telling us He will bless us in the town and in the country is that He will bless us with the fruit of the womb. This blessing is for those who live in the city and for those who live in the country. God will help and provide for us in whichever place we live.

Trust His promises.

Prayer:

"Lord, I thank you for where you have placed us as a family. I rejoice in your provision and I am content. Help us to fulfill your purposes for us in this place at this time of our lives. Amen."

Affirmation:

The safest place for me is in the perfect will of God, no matter where I live.

Day 22

I Am Dangerous!

"But the more they afflicted them, the more they multiplied and grew.
And they were grieved because of the children of Israel"
(Exodus 1:12).

The first chapter of Exodus tells us about the children of Israel living down in Egypt. Verse 7 says, *"And the children of Israel were fruitful, and increased abundantly, and multiplied, and waxed exceeding mighty; and **the land was filled with them**."* They were fulfilling the first commandment that God gave to man. Something powerful always happens when we obey God's commandments. They are not ordinary words to be discarded; they are life-giving decrees.

What happened in Egypt? The children of Israel became *"more and mightier"* than the Egyptians (v. 9). They became a threat to them. And the Egyptians were grieved. The word "grieved" is the Hebrew word *quts* and it means "disgusted, abhorred, horrified, afraid—actually *vomiting* is the primary understanding of the word."

This same Hebrew word is used in another passage where the children of Israel became a threat. In Numbers 22:3 it tells us, *"Moab was sore afraid of the people, because **they were many** and Moab was distressed (quts) because of the children of Israel."* Why was Moab distraught? Because the Israelites were multiplying! When a people multiply, they become scary. When they multiply, they take dominion.

Now, here's the question. Are we, the people of God, a threat to the enemy in our nation today? Sadly, we have to answer No. For the last seven or eight decades, instead of multiplying, God's people have been diminishing. They have turned away from the infallible, immutable Word of God and followed their own desires. They have limited their number of children to the worldwide 1.6 average. They have sacrificed bringing God's children into the world on the altar of careerism and modern culture-ism. And now, the humanists and socialists are taking over.

There are thousands and millions of precious godly offspring who are not here! God has been deprived of His intentions. The world has been deprived of the godly offspring who are meant to fill the nations with His love, righteousness, truth, salvation, wisdom, and justice. And parents themselves have also been deprived.

But, all is not lost. There are a growing number of families who are listening to the heartbeat of God. They are hearing His desire for family and for children. They are turning from their deceptions and opening their hearts to the children that He has destined for them to have, whether it is one or ten! As they obey God's first commandment something amazing is happening. The liberalists are getting scared! They are so horrified, they want to vomit!

Recently a book was published by a radical feminist and published by Beacon Press, which promotes homosexuality and anti-Christian dogma. The author wrote this book to expose Biblical patriarchy and fruitful motherhood. In this book she states that the parents who embrace children are "a movement we ignore at our peril." In a message to Barack Obama, she writes, "Fearless Leader—forget the fundamentalists in Iraq; these prolific Christians are the real bad guys!" In other words, fruitful mothers, embracing the children God wants them to have are dangerous! They are scaring the feminists!

The enemy, who hates life, who comes *"to rob, kill and destroy"* is scared of the godly seed! Mothers who are not deceived by the delusions of Satan, the robber of life, and who believe in God's very first mandate to mankind are dangerous people! Isn't that exciting? You may think you are insignificant as you care for your children in your home each day, but Mother, lift up your eyes! You are doing a powerful work. You are doing God's work. You are dangerous to the enemy. He is scared of you, because he is scared of the godly seed coming into this world who will hate evil and love righteousness, who will destroy the works of the devil and lift up the name of Jesus. And those who walk in deception and follow the devil's ways are scared of you too!

Don't you love being dangerous? Look out! Here we come—holding onto the Word of Life, walking in God's commandments, embracing the godly seed, and training them to be mighty warriors for God who will impact this world and fill it with His glory. Never forget—the more children a godly mother brings into this world . . .

The more scared the liberalists will become!
The more evil will be defeated in the land!
The more the kingdom of God will be advanced!
The more the gospel will be spread across the earth!
The more the image of God will be revealed in the earth!
The more the economy will boom in the land!
The more righteousness and morality will pervade the land!
The more righteous leaders will arise in the nation!
The more justice, honesty, and truth will flood the land!
The more God will be glorified in the earth!

The more the nation will prosper and be blessed!
And the more the statists will fear and tremble!

Keep being dangerous!

Prayer:

"Oh God, please help me to realize the power of motherhood and the power of every child you give me to fulfill your plans in this world. Save me from holding back children whom you have destined to accomplish your mighty works. Amen."

Affirmation:

I am a dangerous woman!

Day 23

My Mission Field

"Then said Jesus unto his disciples, The harvest truly is plenteous, but the laborers are few; pray ye therefore the Lord of the harvest, that he will send forth laborers into his harvest"
(Matthew 9:37-38).

Do you sometimes hanker to be doing some great work for God? You feel as though you are wasting your life in your home. You would love to serve the Lord in some harvest field. Yes, it is true, the harvest is great and the laborers are few. But, why are they few? Because mothers have not understood God's purpose.

Are you looking for an easy path, or do you have a heart to serve God as a missionary? Dear mother, you are already a missionary. God has chosen your specific mission field for you. It is your home and family. You are employed by God to train laborers for His harvest field. You don't raise children and then send them to Bible College to prepare for service. You train them for God's service from the time they are little. They should be ready to labor in the harvest field when they come forth from your home.

Is a missionary's work easy? No, it takes sacrifice. Is motherhood easy? No, but it is eternally worthwhile. It takes everything you've got—all your resources of time, energy and strength—but you will influence nations. It takes committed prayer and intercession, but your prayers will be answered. Many mothering days are exhausting and overwhelming, but you will receive the fruit of your labors and an eternal reward.

Remember, you are not on vacation; you are on the mission field!

Maybe God has only given you one laborer to prepare for Him—that is His plan for you. Maybe He has given you six, or even twelve! Wow, would twelve be too many? Jesus trained twelve disciples who impacted the world. How would you like to train laborers who *"turn the world upside down"*? (Acts 17:6)

What kind of laborers does God want us to faithfully prepare for His service? The following is my vision for our children, grandchildren and future generations. I believe He wants us to prepare children who are . . .

Baby lovers
Blessing imparters
Bible believers
Bible obeyers
Committed laborers in God's harvest
Courageous overcomers
Demon destroyers
Diligent workers
Evil haters
Faithful servers
Fearless soldiers
Freedom fighters
Fruit bearers
God fearers
God lovers
God pleasers
God worshippers
Gospel preachers
Holy Spirit empowered witnesses
Home lovers
Israel supporters
Jesus fanatics
Justice keepers

Life choosers
Light shiners
Liberal threateners
Obedient listeners
Parent honorers
Persecution endurers
Prayer warriors
Princes and Princesses, subjects of a
    royal kingdom
Responsible citizens
Sharp arrows
Tomorrow's leaders
Truth bearers
Truth keepers
Truth lovers
Truth preservers
Truth seekers
Truth speakers
Righteousness lovers
Uncompromising disciples
Valiant conquerors
Wisdom getters and
Zealous servants of the Living God!

Wow! Can you imagine anything more exciting and fulfilling that raising laborers such as these? You couldn't have a greater mission field or a greater vision.

Prayer:

"Thank you, Lord, for showing me my mission field. Help me to serve you faithfully and to raise prepared laborers for your great harvest field. Lord, I am open for you to give me all the laborers you have planned for me to train. Amen."

Affirmation:

I am a full-time missionary, recruiting and training laborers for God's harvest field.

Day 24

Are You Up or Down?

Part 1 – There is lifting up!

*"When men are cast down then thou shalt say, There is lifting up;
and he shall save the humble"*
(Job 22:29).

Are you feeling on top or down in the pits? Perhaps I hear you answer, "Sometimes I'm up and sometimes I'm down! Sometimes I feel great and other times I feel lousy."

I have wonderful news for you. When you are cast down, you don't have to stay down. Even when you are down in the dungeon of despair, you don't have to stay there! **There is lifting up!** Did you receive those wonderful words? Embrace them into your mind and your heart. If you stay in the pit of self-pity or the depths of despair, it is your own choice, for God is waiting to lift you up! This is His name. He is The Lifter Up. What a wonderful and faithful God.

David confesses in Psalm 40:2 TLB, *"He lifted me out of the pit of despair, out from the bog and the mire, and set my feet on a hard, firm path and steadied me as I walked along."* Another time when David was facing great trauma in his life, he confessed, *"But thou, O Lord, art a shield for me; my glory, and the lifter up of mine head"* (Psalm 3:3). Commenting on this Scripture, Charles Spurgeon writes, "There is a lifting up in honor after shame, in health after sickness, in gladness after sorrow, in restoration after a fall, in victory after a temporary defeat; in all these respects the Lord is the lifter up of our head."

You may stumble and fall. This is part of life because not one of us is perfect! But the truth that we must live by is that no matter how many times we fall down, God will lift us up again. Not only will He pull you up out of your slimy pit, but also He will lift up your head. He lifts up your head so you can see clearly again. He lifts up your head to focus on Him instead of on your difficulties. He lifts up your head to behold Him so you will not be ashamed. Psalm 34:5 reminds us that, *"They looked to Him and were radiant, and their faces were not ashamed."*

Can you make the words, "There is lifting up" part of your vocabulary? Say them continually. When you feel you are sliding into gloom or negativity, confess them out loud! When you feel wounded from hurtful words, confess them out loud! When you think there is no hope, confess them out loud. You'll stay up before you can go down!

One reminder: This promise is only for the humble. We can't pull ourselves up. When we think we can do it in our own strength, we'll fail, but when we cry out to God in humility, He'll be waiting. The Amplified Version of Job 22:29 says, *"When they make you low, you will say, There is lifting up; and the humble person He lifts up and saves."* The Living Bible says, *"If you are attacked and knocked down, you will know that there is someone who will lift you up again. Yes, He will save the humble."*

When we get into a habit of continually speaking these words to ourselves, we'll then be able to say to them to others too. We'll say them to our husband. We'll say them to our children. Words of encouragement will roll off our lips to those who are downcast.

God wants you to be on the up instead of on the down.

Prayer:

"Oh God, I thank you that you are the Lifter up of my head. I can't pull myself up. Others can't lift me out of my dregs. You alone can and I trust you to help me. I will not stay down. Thank you that you are my Lifter Up. Amen."

Affirmation:

"I want to live above the world,
Though Satan's darts at me are hurled;
For faith has caught the joyful sound,
The song of saints on higher ground."
~ Johnson Oatman, Jr.

Are You Up or Down?

Part 2 – There is holding up!

*"The steps of a good man are ordered by the Lord,
and he delights in his way. Though he fall, he shall not be utterly cast down;
for the Lord upholds him with his hand"*
(Psalm 37:23-24 RAV). Read also Psalm 17:5.

Not only does God lift us up out of our trough of misery, but He holds us up. And He keeps holding us up as we rest in Him. Isn't it so much better to be up than down?

I am sure you have noticed that when your baby is very upset that he will not be pacified when you sit and hold him. No. He wants to be lifted up and held. He wants you to hold him while you walk around. Sit down. Oh no! He cries again. He wants to be up where you are! He wants to see the world from your point of view. He must feel really out-of-it looking up at us giants. No wonder babies love to be carried in our arms and in baby carriers.

I think it is the same with us. It is easy to grovel when we look at circumstances from our puny point of view. We see the worst. The problems loom large and insurmountable. We can't see our way out. But, God comes. He lifts us up and holds us up. When He holds us, we start to see things from His point of view. We see from an eternal perspective. We receive His wisdom to know what to do. We look down upon our problems instead of being submerged by them.

How does God hold us? He carries us in His strong arms. He holds us with His mighty right arm. When David was being pursued by enemies he confessed to the Lord, *"Your right hand has **held me up**"* (Psalm 18:35). When he was in the wilderness, he cried, *"Your right hand **upholds me**"* (Psalm 63:8).

Now read this wonderful promise in Isaiah 41:10 and 13, *"Fear not, for I am with you; be not dismayed, for I am your God. I will strengthen you. Yes, I will help you. **I will uphold you** with my righteous right hand . . . For I, the Lord your God, will hold your right hand, saying to you, 'Fear not, I will help you.'"*

The word "uphold" in the Hebrew means "to sustain, to maintain, to stay up." God doesn't lift us up to drop us. He holds us up to sustain us. He wants to keep us "stayed up." He does this with His mighty right hand and His hand doesn't get tired.

He carries us and holds us up from the womb to the grave. I love the words of Isaiah 46:3-4, "*Listen to me, O house of Jacob, and all the remnant of the house of Israel, who have been **upheld by me from birth**, who have been carried from the womb: even to your old age, I am he, and even to gray hairs I will carry you! I have made, and I will bear; even I will carry, and will deliver you.*" Read also Isaiah 63:9. The Psalmist affirms this too, "*By you I have been upheld from my birth*" (Psalm 71:6).

Not only does God uphold us with His right hand, but His eternal Word upholds us. The Psalmist confesses in Psalm 119:116, "*Uphold me according to your word, that I may live.*" Do you want to be held up daily? Trust in the Lord and read His Word daily. His life-giving words will sustain you. They will hold you up when everything and everyone is trying to pull you down.

The enemy of your soul, the devil, wants you down. He wants to keep you in the pits. Don't fall for his subtle tactics. Put your hand in the mighty hand of the Lord. Let Him carry you. Feed on His Word and it will hold you up.

Prayer:

"*Oh God, I confess that I cannot hold myself up, but I thank you that you have promised to hold me up. I cling to you and to your life-giving words. Thank you, Lord. Amen.*"

Affirmation:

"A wonderful Savior is Jesus my Lord,
He taketh my burden away;
He holdeth me up, and I shall not be moved,
He giveth me strength for each day."
~ Fanny Crosby

More Scriptures about God Upholding You:
Psalm 17:5; 37:17, 24; 139:9-10 and 145:14.

Day 26

Are You Up or Down?

Part 3a—There is building up!

"As ye therefore have received Christ Jesus the Lord, so walk ye in him: rooted and built up in him, and established in the faith, as ye have been taught, abounding therein with thanksgiving"
(Colossians 2:6-7).

God does not want us to stay down at our lowly level. He wants to bring us up to His life-giving, liberating level. He wants to build us up in Him. He has also shown us how we can be built up.

By Rooting in the Word

Acts 20:32 (TJB) tells us that His gracious words have the power to build us up. *"I commend you to God, and to the Word of His grace that has power to **build you up**."* We can't grow unless we are strongly rooted in God's truth.

By Praying in the Holy Ghost

Jude 20 says, *"But ye, beloved, **building up yourselves** on your most holy faith, praying in the Holy Ghost."*

I know that you know these principles back to front. But there is no way around it. There is no other way to be built up in Christ, in our faith, and strengthened in our inner man than by immersing ourselves in the Word of God and in prayer.

As we are built up, we are then able to build others up. In fact, God has ordained us to be builders. He wants us to be builders of our homes. Proverbs 14:1 personally speaks to women when it says, *"Every wise woman builds her house, but the foolish pulls it down with her hands."*

What does God want us to build? He wants us to build our homes and our families. You will notice that it doesn't say we are to build our careers. If we are wise women, we will put all our effort into building a godly and stable home. Our greatest vision in life will be to build up our marriage and family. We need to get a building mentality. Every time we open our mouths, we should speak words that build up. Every plan we make for the day should be for the purpose of adding to the building program of our home.

The Hebrew word for "build" in Proverbs 14:1 is the Hebrew word, *banah*. There are three aspects to the full understanding of this word.

56

To make, to set up surely, to build

When a builder builds a structure, it grows before one's eyes. When building a home, you excitedly inspect each new development. Building is hard work, but it is creative and stimulating.

Building a family is also hard work but you will be blessed with the fruit of our labors. There is no limit to the creativity. You can fulfill every dream and gifting God has invested in you as you build a strong family for the glory of God.

To repair

This is a very important part of building. All buildings break down and decay. If we do not continually fix and repair, the building will eventually fall down. It is the same with our marriage and family life relationships. We must continually repair with transparency, forgiveness, encouragement, and love. The home-builder knows that, "*Knowledge puffs up, but **love builds up**"* (1 Corinthians 8:1).

To obtain children or bring about an increase in offspring.

This is an unexpected meaning, but very much part of the word. Read Deuteronomy 25:7-9, Ruth 4:11, Psalm 127:1 and Proverbs 14:1 as examples of *banah* being used in this context. Every new child that is received into the family builds the family and makes it grow. The amazing thing is that each new child that comes into the family is not limited to one only. That child will one day have children and his or her children will have children. Each child builds a whole dynasty. In fact, the meaning of the most common Hebrew word for children, "ben," means "the builder of the family name." Every new child helps to build and expand the family, not only in this generation, but also generations to come.

Prayer:

"Oh God, you have shown me clearly that you have purposed for me to be a builder. Please give me a building mentality. Help me to daily build my home by my words and actions. Save me from speaking destructive words. Save me from making decisions that limit or destroy the great building plan you have for our family. Amen."

Affirmation:

I am involved in the greatest building program in the nation—building a godly dynasty!

Day 27

Are You Up or Down?

Part 3b — There is building up!

"Through wisdom a house is built, and by understanding it is established"
(Proverbs 24:3).

A builder cannot build a home without tools. He needs a saw, hammer, spirit level, and plumb line, etc. We also need tools in order to build a godly home. We cannot build without the tools of love, forgiveness, encouragement, understanding, positivity, prayer, and intercession and so on. However, the Word of God tells us that the main building tool we need is wisdom.

Proverbs 9:1 says, *"Wisdom has built her house, she has hewn out her seven pillars."* The tool of wisdom builds seven pillars that make a marriage and home strong and durable. What are these seven pillars? I believe they are recorded for us in James 3:17, *"But the wisdom that is from above is first pure, then peaceable, gentle, easy to be entreated, full of mercy and good fruits, without partiality, and without hypocrisy."*

A pillar is a strong support to hold up a building. As we seek to build these pillars into our marriage and family, we will build a home that is strong and secure, a home that will stand the trials and storms that will inevitably buffet us.

1. The Pillar of Purity

The word "pure" in the Greek is *hagnos* which means "freedom from defilements or impurities, pure in body, mind and spirit, unpolluted, clean, modest, and chaste." As we build the pillar of purity, we guard our home from all defiling movies, literature, Internet, and anything that would taint the minds of our children. God is looking for clean minds, clean hearts, and clean homes where He can dwell. Hebrews 12:14 says, *"Follow peace with all men, and holiness (hagnos), without which no man shall see the Lord."*

Continually pray for the purifying power of the Holy Spirit to blow through your home. Regularly check your home for immoral books, DVDs, toys, pictures, and ornaments that can infiltrate your home. God commands us in Deuteronomy 7:25-26, *"Nor shall you bring an abomination into your house, lest you be doomed to destruction like it; but you shall utterly detest it and utterly abhor it, for it is an accursed thing."* Read also Deuteronomy 18:9-14, Psalm 24:3-5; 51:10; 73:1 and Isaiah 1:16.

2. The Pillar of Peacemaking

In every hurtful situation, there is always an opportunity to make peace. We can choose to thrust the sword in further, demanding the last say, but the end result is destruction. The hardest thing to do is to give a soft answer, respond with forgiveness, and make steps toward peace, but this will build a strong marriage and home. This pillar will fill your home with blessing. Jesus Himself told us this in Matthew 5:9, *"Blessed are the peacemakers: for they shall be called the children of God."* Are you building the peacemaking pillar in your home?

3. The Pillar of Gentleness

This seems a paradox doesn't it? How can gentleness be a strong pillar? David confessed in Psalm 18:35, *"Thy gentleness has made me great."* A gentle spirit is very precious in the sight of God. It is priceless in the home and very precious to a husband, too (1 Peter 3:4). Man's wisdom tells us to be self-assertive. The wisdom from above tells us to cultivate a gentle spirit. The word literally means, "forbearing." In other words, we should react with gentleness rather than sharply and rudely when our children or husband make us mad. This pillar will add divine strength to you, your marriage, and your family.

One evening our daughter and husband and their seven children (they now have ten) sat around our table for supper. As we enjoyed our meal together, each one of us, including the children, shared a new revelation that God had given us. Because I was thinking about building pillars, I asked the children, "How do you think we can build a pillar of gentleness in the home?" Ten-year-old Zadok responded, "No harsh words, no yelling, no arguing, and no negativity to one another." Five-year-old Crusoe answered, "No rudeness to one another." They had the right answers, didn't they?

Prayer:

"Oh God, thank you for this great revelation that I am a pillar builder. Fill me with your divine wisdom as I walk softly before you in my home. Help me to build with your wisdom, not the wisdom of this world that is earthly, sensual, and devilish. Save me from being tainted by this humanistic wisdom for I want to build godly pillars. Amen."

Affirmation:

I am a pillar builder!

Day 28

Are You Up or Down?

Part 3c – There is building up!

"Let us rise up and build"
(Nehemiah 2:18).

Let's discover the rest of the pillars of wisdom.

4. The Pillar of Yieldedness

This looks like a weak pillar doesn't it? But, not in God's eyes. A willingness to yield takes strength. It builds a strong pillar. Here are some different translations:

"easy to be entreated" (KJB).
"willing to yield" (RAV, NLT).
"approachable" (JBP).
"open to reason" (NEB, RSV, CJB), and
"submissive" (NIV).

Are you resisting your husband's leading? This will weaken your home. As you yield, you will build your marriage. You will build a godly pillar into your home and your children will learn from watching you. Your attitude will affect the generations to come.

5. The Pillar of Mercy and Good Fruits

God is a merciful and forgiving God. Because He is merciful, He wants to reveal His mercy through us. He wants our homes to be filled with compassion, forgiveness, and the good fruits of His Holy Spirit—love, joy, peace, longsuffering, gentleness, goodness, faithfulness, meekness, and self-control (Galatians 5: 22-23). The Message translates it, *"Overflowing with mercy and blessings."* Wouldn't you like this to be your testimony? We must have judgment, discipline, and order in a home, but we sure need mercy, too, don't we?

"How often do I have to forgive someone who sins against me? asked Peter. "Seven times?"

"Oh no!" replied Jesus. "Seventy times seven!" That's 490 times! It actually means an indefinite number, as many times as someone hurts you (Matthew 18:21-22)! We certainly have plenty of opportunities to build a huge pillar of forgiveness and mercy, don't we? When we refuse to show mercy and forgive, we tear down our marriage and home. When we forgive again and again, we build up this mighty pillar.

Did you have to forgive many times today? Perhaps you'll have to do it again tomorrow! Don't give up. Remember, this is an endless command from our Lord and Savior. God extends His mercies freshly and newly to us every morning (Lamentations 3:22-23). In the same way, with His grace, we show mercy and forgiveness each new day.

How strong is this pillar in your home?

6. The Pillar of Impartiality

How we need the wisdom from above to act with fairness and justness. It is easy to see things from a wrong perspective when we use our own wisdom. Cry out for God's wisdom as you guide and discipline your children.

7. The Pillar of Genuineness

There is no hypocrisy in God's wisdom. There should be none in ours either. The word in James 3:17 is "unfeigned" which means "genuine, sincere, not counterfeit, and not hypocritical." Down in Australia, they call someone who can be trusted and who is truly genuine, "fair dinkum" or "true blue." This is how our children should see us. They should see that our faith and love are genuine and that we act at home the same way that we act at church on Sunday! The easiest way to turn your children away from God is for them to see hypocrisy in your lives. The greatest way to lead them to God is for them to see that you are "true blue."

Tune your heart to God's wisdom as you daily build these seven pillars into your home and marriage.

Prayer:

"Oh God, please help me to be 'true blue.' I want my children to see that my faith is genuine. Help to wake each morning with a building mentality so that my every word and action will build up my home. Save me from being destructive and pulling down. Amen."

Affirmation:

I've begun building a godly home and I will finish my course. I will not give up halfway through, no matter how difficult the obstacles.

Day 29

Are You Up or Down?

Part 4 – There is rising up!

"But God, who is rich in mercy, because of his great love with which he loved us, even when we were dead in trespasses, made us alive together with Christ (by grace you have been saved), and raised us up together, and made us sit together in the heavenly places in Christ Jesus"
(Ephesians 2:4-6).

Are you living it up? Come on now; let's get with it. God is into the "living it up" lifestyle. He not only lifts us up, holds us up, builds us up but He also raises us up! One day, we are going to be raised up to the eternal realm. You can read some of the Scriptures that tell us of this glorious hope in 1 Corinthians 6:14,15:49-54 and 1 Thessalonians 4:16.

However, even before God fulfils this ultimate promise to us, He raises us up in this life. Yes, right now. When Christ died, we died with him; when He was buried, we were buried with Him; when He ascended, we were raised with Him and now positionally sit with Him in heavenly places. This seems too awesome to believe, doesn't it? We may not be experiencing it, but it is written in the Word. It is fact.

How can we experience this revelation truth? By abiding in Christ. Notice that this does not happen to us on our own. It is only as we are in Him. And one other thing: We have to be buried first! Jesus died and was buried before He was raised to reign at the right hand of the Father. We also have to die to our flesh and be buried before we can live in resurrection life.

Dear precious mother, from what position do you run your home? From the bottom of the barrel? Are you looking up at all you have to do? Are you submerged by all your worries and concerns? Or, do you run your home from your legal position (which has nothing to do with your feelings) of sitting together with Christ at the right hand of the throne of God? In this position, you look down on your problems. You have victory over them. In this position in Christ, all things are under your feet. From this location, you take dominion over all the inroads of the enemy that would seek to spoil your marriage and your home. Read Ephesians 1:17-23 and Romans 6:4.

You were raised with Christ, not only to sit with Him, but also to reign with Him. Let this incredible truth sink into your soul. You were raised to reign! You were raised to live in resurrection life. In Christ you reign over all evil principalities and powers. In Christ you reign over all negativity, depression, laziness, and sin in your home.

F.B. Meyer writes, "Abide in Him, and you are by necessity an inhabitant of these heavenly places, wherever your earthly lot may be cast . . . Not one foe can overcome us so long as we are in abiding fellowship with our risen Lord. If the 'together' of the inner life is maintained, the 'together' of victory is secure."

How sad that we grovel around when we have actually been raised up together with Christ. We live the shallow life according to our feelings rather than reigning in Christ.

Can I entice you to live in your ascended state? Can I remind you that you have been raised to live in resurrection life? Can I encourage you to manage your home from your legal position of authority in Christ? It is your legal right.

Why stay down in the dumps when God has raised you up?

Prayer:

"Oh Lord, I thank you that because you have been raised from the dead, I have been raised up with you. Even though it is hard for me to believe with my human mind, I thank you that I am seated with you at the right hand of the Father. Help me to grasp this awesome truth. Teach me, Lord, to abide in you moment by moment, and live my life from my legal position in Christ. Amen."

Affirmation:

I have been raised to reign!

More Promises:

He raises up the poor out of the dust (1 Samuel 2:8; Psalm 113:7-8).
He raises up those that are bowed down (Psalm 146:8).
He raises up the sick when we call for the elders of the church to pray and anoint with oil (James 5:14-15).

Day 30

Tinkling with Joy

"And it (the robe) shall be upon Aaron to minister: and his sound (tinkling of bells) shall be heard when he goes in unto the holy place before the Lord" (Exodus 28:35).

We read in Exodus 28 about the garments that God ordained the High Priest to wear. They were garments for *"glory and beauty"* (v. 2). On the robe of the High Priest, God instructed them to make blue, purple, and scarlet pomegranates with golden bells in between them, *"a golden bell and a pomegranate, a golden bell and a pomegranate, upon the hem of the robe round about"* (v. 34). One Bible commentator says there may have been 72 bells and pomegranates around the hem of the garment.

Every part of the High Priest's garments had spiritual significance. Because God has made us "kings and priests" unto Him, they have spiritual significance in our lives, too. Read 1 Peter 2:5,9; Revelation 1:6; 5:10; and 20:6.

Because pomegranates are filled with seeds, they speak of fruitfulness. Wherever we walk, in our home or out in the supermarket, we should continually drop seeds of God's truth, love, and peace.

What comes to your mind when you think of little bells tinkling? Yes, a smile comes to your face. You think of joy and gladness. God wanted to be refreshed by sounds of joy as Aaron fulfilled his priestly duties in the holy place. I am sure God also wants to hear the tinkling of joy as we go about our motherly duties in our home.

God's picture of a mother in the home is one who is filled with joy. Psalm 113:9 says, *"He makes the barren woman to keep house and to be a joyful mother of children."* As a child I remember my mother always singing in the home. What happiness it brought to my childhood heart. These were the days when mothers sang in their homes and men whistled as they walked or cycled to work. Women enjoyed being in their homes. They didn't hanker to be out in the workforce. And they sang. I know we live a much faster pace of life today, but as we make our life more and more in the heart of the home, the song will return.

Did you notice that the tinkling bells were on the hem of the garment? They are part of the daily grind. This joy is not in the heavenlies, but touches the realities of our daily life. It is easily accessible to our little ones toddling around the home.

As you wake each morning, put on your priestly garments of holiness and joy. Make sure the bells are tinkling on your hem as you go out to your kitchen to prepare breakfast for your children. Start the breakfast with praise. Instead of the usual grace, hold hands together and sing a song of thanks before you eat. Tell your children that you love being their mother. Tell them you are glad God has given you another day to enjoy together.

Keep the bells tinkling all day. Turn every sigh into a Hallelujah! When things go wrong, praise the Lord instead of whining. Practice this until it becomes the habit of your life.

Here are some more word pictures about tinkling in your home . . .

Exodus 15:2, *"The Lord is my strength and song, and He is become my salvation . . . and I will prepare Him a habitation."* How do we make our home a habitation for God? By filling our home with songs of salvation. By humming a tune as we wash the dishes or prepare the meals. By praising instead of sighing when we have to clean up another mess.

Psalm 118:15, *"The voice of rejoicing and salvation is in the tabernacles (homes) of the righteous."* What is the voice in your home? Is it one of sour silence? Groanings and complainings? Or the tinkling of joy?

Psalm 119:54, "Thy statutes have been my songs in the house of my pilgrimage."

Isaiah 32:13, "The houses of joy . . ." In this Scripture, God is pronouncing a judgment on all the homes of Israel because of their sin. But, do you notice how God describes their homes? He calls them *"houses of joy."*

Keep the bells tinkling.

Prayer:

"Father God, I pray that you will give me contentment in my home, knowing this is where you have planted me. Help me to delight in my home and mothering my children. May my children see me tinkling with joy as I walk in my home, even when doing the most mundane household chores. Thank you for the power of the Holy Spirit which is working this out in me. Amen."

Affirmation:

I am turning my sighs into songs,
My miseries into melodies.

Day 31

Wear the Right Clothes!

"Put off, concerning your former conduct, the old man which was corrupt according to the deceitful lusts and be renewed in the spirit of your mind, and that you put on the new man which was created according to God, in righteousness and true holiness"
(Ephesians 4:22-24).

When you were born again by the Spirit of God, you received a new wardrobe. It is a very expensive wardrobe, paid for by the precious blood of Christ. You have so many beautiful garments hanging in this wardrobe. You have lovely dresses of love, joy, peace, longsuffering gentleness, goodness, faithfulness, meekness, and self-control (Galatians 5:22-23). You have delightful garments of tender mercies, kindness, humility, meekness, longsuffering, forbearance, and forgiveness (Colossians 3:12-17).

The strange thing is that although we have this expensive wardrobe, we don't always bother to wear the clothes. We are so used to our old shabby clothes of the flesh. We feel more comfortable in them. They feel familiar, so we stick with them instead of trying out our new wardrobe. To put on a beautiful dress of gentleness or patience seems foreign because we are not used to wearing them. But they belong to you! They are yours!

Imagine if your husband purchased a very expensive dress for you. You couldn't believe how stylish it was. But you never wore it. You thought it was too good for you. How would your husband feel when he paid so much for it and wanted to be proud of you wearing it?

I wonder how God feels when He gives us this glorious wardrobe, purchased at an enormous price, and we never wear the garments?

God freely gives us these garments, but He doesn't put them on us. He tells us to PUT THEM ON! Ephesians 4:24 tells us to *"Put on the new man."* I love the J. B. Philipp's translation which says, *"Fling off the dirty clothes of the old way of living . . . And **put on the clean fresh clothes of the new life.**"*

Make sure you put on a new garment each morning. Have you had a lousy night with the baby awake all night? Are you going through a fiery ordeal? Put on your garment of praise (Isaiah 61:1-3).

Let me tell you a secret. You won't feel like putting it on. You'd much rather put on your dirty old dress of grumbling and complaining. But, do it by faith. Don't worry about your feelings. Start praising and thanking the Lord. As you do it by faith, you will actually wear it.

You can change garments as you need them throughout the day. Are the children getting on your nerves? You feel your anger rising. Quick! Change into your garment of long-suffering or patience. Put it on by faith. Thank the Lord for His patience which is in you because He lives in you.

You are starting to get cranky and yell at everyone because things are getting on top of you? Change into your garment of gentleness. Thank the Lord for His gentle spirit which lives in you. This is the new man. It is, *"Christ in you the hope of glory"* (Colossians 1:27). He lives in you now. All these beautiful garments belong to you. All you have to do is wear them by faith!

Strip off your old shabby garments. Wear your new ones each day. Live in them. Let Christ live His beautiful life through you.

Prayer:

"Thank you, Lord, for all the beautiful garments that you have given to me. I am sick of my old rags. They look so ugly to everyone. Help me to put on your beautiful new garments which reveal your beautiful life in me. Amen."

Affirmation:

I may have little in my literal wardrobe, but I have access to the most glorious garments in my spiritual wardrobe.

Day 32

Bigger Than You!

"He brought you out of Egypt with his Presence, with his mighty power,
*driving out from before you nations **greater and mightier** than you"*
(Deuteronomy 4:37-38).

Isn't God so good to give us a fresh new day every morning? Yesterday is gone. Perhaps you felt like a total failure yesterday. Maybe everything went wrong. Forget it. Today is a new day. It is a new day for you to train and nurture your children for the destiny that God has planned for them. Don't worry about all you have to accomplish. Instead, keep the eyes of your heart upon the Lord. He is your Sufficiency. He is your Strength. He is your Rock. He is the God who is Enough. He is the One who has given you this mighty task of training your children for His glory. Because He has given you this mandate, He will help you carry it out. You don't have to do it on your own. He wants to work with you if you will let Him.

God has promised us in Psalm 55:22 that if we release the weight of our burden on to the Lord, He will take it and sustain us. Isn't that a wonderful promise? Why carry the burden yourself when you can cast it upon the Lord?

I admit that God has given you a big undertaking in motherhood. In fact, it is such an important assignment that it takes every effort of your being—physically, emotionally, mentally, and spiritually. It's not for the fainthearted. It is the greatest calling in the nation. You are training God's task force. You are training the generation that could usher in the coming of the Lord. It's a huge task, but you have a powerful God behind you. With God you can do things that are bigger than you.

God told the children of Israel to go into the Promised Land and drive out the nations that were *"greater and mightier"* than they were. Deuteronomy 9:1-3 says, *"Hear, O Israel: You are to cross over the Jordan today, and go in to dispossess nations **greater and mightier** than yourself, cities great and fortified up to heaven, a people great and tall, the descendants of the Anakim* (who were giants), *whom you know, and of whom you heard it said, 'Who can stand before the descendants of Anak?' Therefore understand today that the Lord your God is he who goes over before you as a consuming fire. He will destroy them and bring them down before you; so you shall drive them out and destroy them quickly, as the Lord has said to you."* Also read Deuteronomy 11:22-24.

God commanded them to do something that was bigger than they were! It was impossible to accomplish this task with their own strength. But He knew that they could do it, because He was with them.

Dear mother, do you feel that this job of motherhood is too much for you? Do you feel it is bigger than you can handle? Perhaps you are homeschooling and you feel totally overwhelmed. You don't have to do it on your own. God is with you! Thank Him that He is with you.

Remember . . .

With God you can do things that are bigger and mightier than you!

Prayer:

Dear God, so many times I feel everything is too much for me. But I thank you that you are with me. You are my Strength. You are my Help. You are my Deliverer! I thank you that when you are with me I can do things that are greater and mightier than my natural strength. Lord, I claim your strength today. Thank you in Jesus' name. Amen."

Affirmation:

I walk in the strength of the Lord.

Day 33

Born to Look Up

"I will look up"
(Psalm 5:3).

It is an amazing fact, yet hard to comprehend, that we are created in the image and likeness of God. We were created to reveal what God is like through our nature, but also through our physical body. God designed our body to function in the way He functions without a body. Although God does not have a body, He can see, hear, smell, touch, and speak, just as He created us to do. Whenever God appeared visibly to mankind, he came in the form of a human body. And wondrously, God prepared a human body for His own precious Son, *"made in the likeness of men"* just as man was made *"in the likeness of God"* (Philippians 2:7 and Genesis 1:26).

Another interesting factor is the way God created our physical body. He did not create us to walk on all fours like animals, but created us with an upright posture. We were born to look up, to have an upward gazing countenance. God did not intend his highest creation to grovel in the dust and to be bowed down with depression and defeat. He created us with an erect carriage, a posture that enables us to look up to Him, a posture that gives expression to freedom and positivity.

God wants you to walk with your head held high. He wants you to turn your thoughts to Him, your heart to Him and your face to Him.

Leviticus 26:13 says, *"I am the Lord your God, which brought you forth out of the land of Egypt, that ye shall not be their bondmen; and I have broken the bands of your yoke, and made you go upright"*

The RSV says, *"Made you walk erect."*

The NLT says, *"So you can walk free with your heads held high."*

The children of Israel walked erect with their heads held high because they were free men, no longer slaves to Egypt. Not only did God create us free, with the command to rule and reign, but when sin came in and we became enslaved to its power, God sent a Redeemer to deliver us. Once again, through the power of the cross, we are set free to walk with our heads held high.

No room for downcast looks!

The psalmist says in Psalm 34:5, *"They looked unto him and were radiant, and their faces were not ashamed."* The Knox translation says, *"Ever look to Him . . . no room for downcast looks."* When your head sags, He is waiting to lift it up. You will never be ashamed when you look up to the Lord. Your face will brighten. Make it the habit of your life. It is what you were created to do.

We are often encouraged in the Psalms to wait upon the Lord. Did you know that this word also means to look to the Lord? Some scholars believe that "wait" *(quvah)* has two roots:

1) To bind together by twisting, to be joined

2) To expect, to look for patiently, hope, be confident. This Hebrew word *quvah* is translated "wait" over 30 times, but the same word is translated "look" over 14 times.

Psalm 27:14 says, *"Wait (quvah) on the Lord, be of good courage and he shall strengthen thine heart, wait, I say on the Lord."* If you want your heart strengthened, you must look up to the Lord in expectancy. This is what gives courage to your heart, physically and spiritually.

Check your posture today. Are you walking erect? Is your head held high? Is your face upturned to the Lord?

Prayer:

"Father, I thank you that you created me to look up to you. You are my strength and motivation for living. Amen."

Affirmation:

I look to God and worries cease,
Now my heart is filled with peace!

Day 34

Me, Brutish? Surely Not!

*"Whoso loveth instruction loveth knowledge: but he that hateth
reproof is brutish"*
(Proverbs 12:1).

Brutish." What an ugly word! I was challenged when I read this Scripture in my daily reading. I certainly didn't think of myself as brutish. But, the Word of God is powerful and the Holy Spirit convicted me that I am guilty.

I don't like being reproved, do you? I don't like being told what to do all the time. There are many times when my husband reproves me in order to get me in line. I don't always like it. My first reaction is to resist on the inside even if I don't show it on the outside. I now realize this is brutish.

Sometimes my husband asks me to do something and I think, "I'm busier than you are." My flesh does not like being ordered around. Once again, I realize this is brutish. I certainly don't want to be brutish and so I repent and ask the Lord to give me a soft and responsive heart.

It's so easy to react in the flesh. The flesh does not like interruptions. The flesh does not like being reproved. The flesh does not like being told what to do. But are we going to walk according the to the flesh, or according to the Spirit of God who lives within us?

Many modern translations of Proverbs 12:1 read, *"He who hates reproof is stupid."* "Stupid" is not as strong a word as "brutish" but it still reveals that it is an immature reaction. Children do not like to be reproved. It takes maturity to receive reproof with a soft and open heart. Reproof brings us into a larger place in our lives and causes us to grow into the likeness of Jesus.

The psalmist cries out in Psalm 141:5, *"Let the righteous strike me; it shall be a kindness. And let him reprove me; it shall be as excellent oil; let my head not refuse it."* The psalmist states that receiving reproof is like receiving the "oil of gladness" that was poured on the head on festive occasions. He does not resist it because he knows it will bless him and make him greater. The Living Bible says, *"If they reprove me, it is medicine!"*

The Hebrew word for "brutish" is *baar* and means, "to be consumed." If we do not allow the Spirit of God to soften our hearts, in order to receive rebuke and admonition, we will end up being consumed with our own ways and desires. We will become eaten up with hurt and bitterness. We will be stubborn wives who ultimately destroy our marriage. We will be frustrated mothers for we will produce children with the same brutish spirit who will not receive reproof and instruction. Our children will receive rebuke and admonition in the same way that we receive it from our husband, or from other people.

Proverbs 9:8-9 says, "*Reprove not a scorner, lest he hate thee: rebuke a wise man, and he will love thee. Give instruction to a wise man, and he will be yet wiser: teach a just man, and he will increase in learning.*"

Proverbs 10:17 says, "*He who refuses reproof goes astray.*"

Isaiah 66:2 says, "*But to this man will I look; even to him that is poor and of a contrite spirit, and who trembles at my word.*"

One of the greatest blessings we can allow the Lord to work in us is a soft and sensitive heart toward Him, toward our husband, and toward others. It is also one of the greatest prayers we can pray for our children, that they also will have soft hearts to hear and obey the Lord.

Let's cast every tendency to brutishness out of our hearts.

Prayer:

"Oh God, please save me from having a brutish spirit. Oh Spirit of God, please move upon my heart and work in me a contrite and humble spirit. Give me a heart that can receive reproof with joy, knowing that this will enable me to grow into a larger place in my walk with You. Thank you, Lord."

Affirmation:

I will not resist admonition, but embrace it with joy.

Further Study:

Go to page 215 to check more Scriptures about listening to instruction.
Go to page 217 to check God's attitude toward a prideful spirit.

Day 35

Which Camp?

*"Unto the church of God which is at Corinth, to them that are sanctified in Christ Jesus, called to be saints, with all that in every place **call upon the name of Jesus Christ our Lord**"*
(1 Corinthians 1:2).

Did you know that the early Christians were referred to as those who *"call upon the name of the Lord"*? You can read more references in Acts 9:14, 21 and 2 Timothy 2:22.

Do you think God's people have this testimony today? Is it such a normal habit of our lives that the ungodly see this as our habitual characteristic? Do our neighbors know us as people who call upon the name of the Lord? How many times during the day do we acknowledge the Lord and call upon His name?

It started in the beginning. While the generations of Cain were going after material pursuits and worldly business another godly line was born to Adam and Eve. Genesis 4:25-26 says, *"And Adam knew his wife again; and she bare a son, and called his name Seth: For God, said she, hath appointed me another seed instead of Abel, whom Cain slew. And to Seth, to him also there was born a son; and he called his name Enos: **then began men to call upon the name of the Lord**."* History says that Enos was the first of eight preachers of righteousness, of whom Noah was the eighth.

This new generation began to call upon the name of the Lord in prayer, thanksgiving, and worship. This is when they began public worship. They became **known** as people who called upon the Lord.

It is this way of life that distinguishes us as the people of God from the heathen. The ungodly do not call upon the Lord. The godly do. This decides which camp we belong to.

Recently I was challenged by reading Jeremiah 10:25, *"Pour thy fury upon the heathen that know thee not, **and** upon the **families** that call not on thy name."* This Scripture is talking about **families**. Not churches, but families. Therefore we had better take notice because it relates to us. It is convicting to realize that families who do not gather together to call upon the name of the Lord are equated with the heathen! Ouch!

How many "Christian" families are actually heathen families? They do not gather together for prayer and worship from one day to the next. Life is too busy. The program is chock full from morning 'till night. What distinguishes them from the worldly?

I, too, find that life is busy from morning until night. Therefore, I find we have to **make** times to call upon the Lord. If we don't, it doesn't happen. On our home, we have established Morning and Evening devotions where we come together as a family to read the Word and call upon the Lord. We don't allow any interruption to interfere with this habit. For if we do not do it, we cannot confess we are the people of God. God's people call upon His name.

What does this word "call" mean? It is not a mumbling prayer or a quick, "God bless our family today" and go on our merry way. The Hebrew word is *qara* which means, "to cry out, call out loudly, to roar, to summon God's aid."

When we call upon the Lord we show our dependence upon Him. We know we cannot make it in our own strength. Jeremiah 10:23 says, *"The way of man is not in himself: it is not in man that walketh to direct his steps."* We need God to show us the way.

The morals of our nation are deteriorating fast! We stand guilty before God for the murder of over 50 million babies since Roe v. Wade. Atheism, immorality, and homosexuality, are rife. It may not be long before our nation's financial resources fail. How can we go blindly on while our nation goes down the road of wickedness? Do we not have any heart to cry out to God. The hour is urgent for families to come together and to pray, night and morning. God has promised that when we humble ourselves and cry out to Him that He will hear us and save our land (2 Chronicles 7:14).

Will we as families pay the sacrifice to see God's deliverance or will we go blindly on our merry way?

Prayer:

"Oh Father, please save me from living like the heathen. Please help us as a family to make specific times to call upon your name for our own salvation and the salvation of this nation. Amen."

Affirmation:

We will be known as a family that calls upon the name of the Lord.

Go to www.aboverubies.org and search for THE MORNING AND EVENING PRINCIPLE to read more about this biblical habit.

Day 36

Choices Have Consequences

"Be not deceived; God is not mocked: for whatsoever a man soweth, that shall he also reap"
(Galatians 6:7).

As parents, we carry a great responsibility. We can no longer live to ourselves. It is an awesome fact that every decision we make will not only affect our destiny, but also the destiny of our children, grandchildren, and the continuing generations.

Our children were all affected by our decision to move from New Zealand to Australia back in 1982, and then to USA in 1991.

Fortunately, our children are all glad we made those decisions. Because we lived in Australia for nearly 10 years, our three sons married Australian girls. When we moved to America, our three daughters married Americans! Our decisions certainly affected the futures of our children and determined the precious grandchildren that we have today.

Every choice, big or small, on a day-to-day basis or long-term goal, influences our children. How we need to listen to God's voice so that He will lead us in the right direction.

I was very challenged by reading the story of Lot. Abraham and Lot lived and worked together for years. The day came when their flocks and goods increased so greatly that they needed to separate. Abraham gave Lot the opportunity to choose first. He chose the plains, the easy way, and pitched his tent toward Sodom. Eventually he was lured right into the evil city and lived there. The choice he made eventually caused sorrow and heartache to himself, death to most of his family, and devastating consequences to the succeeding generations.

Lot lost all his possessions—his home, his wife who was turned to a pillar of salt, most of his family members, and his business. More appalling was the fact that the children who were born to him by incest were the originators of the Ammonites and the Moabites. Lot's generations became the enemies of Abraham's descendents! What devastating consequences! Instead of producing godly generations, Lot produced ungodly generations.

You can read about it in Genesis 19:37-38, *"Thus were both the daughters of Lot with child by their father. And the firstborn bare a son, and called his name Moab: the same is the father of the Moabites this day. And the younger, she also bare a son, and called his name Benammi: the same is the father of the children of Ammon unto this day.*"

It was not an evil man that made this choice. 2 Peter 2:6-8 says that Lot was a just and righteous man, "*oppressed with the filthy conduct of the wicked . . .*" A righteous man made a wrong decision! May God help us to make the right choices.

We need to make every choice in the light of eternity and in the light of the generations to come. We must not base our decision on how the outcome will affect us now. We must think of what the effect will be upon our children and future generations. This will help us to make right decisions.

Prayer:

"*Oh Lord, you have promised to be my Guide, even unto death. I look to you to guide me in all my decisions, the little ones and the big ones. Help me to stay close to you so I can hear your voice saying, 'This is the way, walk ye in it.' Help me to hear your voice louder than the voices in the world that seek to influence me. Thank you, Lord. Amen.*"

Affirmation:

I am making my decisions in the light of eternity.

Day 37

Covenant Keepers

Part 1 – I cannot break covenant!

*"I have brought you unto the land which I sware unto your fathers;
and I said, **I will never break my covenant with you**"*
(Judges 2:1). Read also Joshua 21:45; 23:14; 2 Chronicles 6:14;
Nehemiah 1:5 and Psalm 89:33-35.

God is a covenant-maker and a covenant-keeper. He makes everlasting covenants. Here are a few of many Scriptures that tell about His everlasting covenants: Genesis 17:7,19; Deuteronomy 7:8-9; 2 Samuel 23:5, 1 Chronicles 16:15-18; Isaiah 55:3 and Jeremiah 32:40.

Every covenant God makes He keeps. God says that He would have to do away with the laws of nature—day and night would have to cease and the waves of the sea no longer roll before He would break His covenant. The mountains would have to depart and the hills be removed. In fact, heaven and earth would have to disappear before His words could fail! Read these wonderful promises: Isaiah 54:10; Jeremiah 31:35-37; 33:20-21; 25-26 and Matthew 24:35.

Let's read another utterance from the mouth of God—Psalm 89:34, *"My covenant will I not break, nor alter the thing that is gone out of my lips."* Because we are His people, God expects us to have this same covenant-keeping attitude. Because covenant-keeping is part of God's character, He notices when covenants are broken. We see an example of this during the reign of King David. 2 Samuel 21:1 tells us, *"Now there was a famine in the days of David for three years, year after year; and David inquired of the Lord. And the Lord answered, 'It is because of Saul and his bloodthirsty house, because he killed the Gibeonites.'"*

Many years before, Joshua and the elders of Israel made a covenant with the Gibeonites. After the great victories of Jericho and Ai, the Gibeonites feared for their lives and thought of a way of deceiving the Israelis. They sent ambassadors to Joshua wearing worn-out clothing and patched shoes, and carrying old cracked wineskins and dry moldy bread to pretend they had come from a far distant country. The trick worked. Joshua forgot to ask the Lord about it and they signed a peace treaty. Three days later, Joshua and the elders of Israel found out that the Gibeonites were actually close neighbors! But, they had made a covenant and therefore it could not be changed.

Years and years later, when Saul became king, he slaughtered some of the Gibeonites. God took notice. He didn't do anything about it then. God always does things in His own time. But the breaking of this covenant had to be avenged. When David went to the Gibeonites, they demanded David give them seven descendents of Saul who they hung before the Lord. Only then did the famine cease.

We see another example of covenant-keeping in this same chapter of 2 Samuel 21. When David gave Saul's descendents to the Gibeonites to be hung, he made sure that he spared *"Mephibosheth, the son of Jonathan, the son of Saul, **because of the Lord's oath that was between them**, between David and Jonathan, the son of Saul."*

It is interesting that David and Jonathan's oath was called "the Lord's oath." It not only belonged to David, and Jonathan, it belonged to God. 1 Samuel 23:18 says that when David and Jonathan covenanted *"they two made a covenant **before the Lord**"* (1 Samuel 18:3, 20:8,14-17, 42). God aligns Himself with covenants. When we break covenant with people, we break covenant with Him too.

Marriage could also be called, "The Lord's oath." It is a covenant that we make before God and before witnesses "until death do us part." It is made in the name of the Lord. God sees it, He hears it, and He takes note. And He also takes note when it is broken.

In Malachi 2:13-16 God tells the husbands that He no longer regards their offerings. When they asked, "Why?" He replied, *"Because the Lord has been witness between you and the wife of your youth, to whom you have been faithless, although she is your companion and **your wife by covenant**."*

Proverbs 2:17 talks about the wife *"who forsakes the husband of her youth and forgets the **covenant of her God**."*

God reminds the husband and the wife that marriage is a covenant. In Proverbs 2:17 He reminds the wife that her covenant is not only between her and her husband, but it is also a covenant with God, a God who does not forget covenants.

Prayer:

"Oh God, I thank you that you are a covenant-keeping God. You are true to all your promises. You never fail. Please give me your strength and enabling to also be a covenant-keeper. Amen."

Affirmation:

I am destined to be a covenant-keeper!

Day 38

Covenant Keepers

Part 2 – I cannot break my word!

*"This is the thing which the Lord has commanded. If a man vow a vow unto the Lord, or swear an oath to bind his soul with a bond; **he shall not break his word**, he shall do according to all that proceeds out of his mouth"* (Numbers 30:1-2).

We are discovering that marriage is not only a covenant between the husband and wife but also a covenant with God. And God wants us to be covenant keepers. This makes the marriage contract far more serious than society looks upon it today.

"But you don't know how difficult my marriage situation is," you reply. Let's look at another example in the Word of God which is given for our admonition.

It is the story of Jephthah, one of the judges of Israel. When he went out to war against the Ammonites he made a vow to the Lord that if God gave him the victory he would sacrifice to the Lord the first thing to come out of his house on his return. Tragically, the first one to come out of his home was his beloved daughter, his only child. Jephthah was devastated. *"When he saw her, he tore his clothes in anguish. 'My daughter!' he cried out. 'My heart is breaking! What a tragedy that you came out to greet me. For I have made a vow to the Lord and **cannot take it back**"* (Judges 11:34-35 NLT).

What a distraught father! But, he had made a vow and could not take it back. He could not annul it. The Israelites understood the solemnity of vows and covenants. In this situation, he did not sacrifice his daughter's life as that was against God's laws, but instead he sacrificed her to be a virgin all her life (which was as bad as death for an Israelite daughter).

It cost Jephthah unbelievable heartache to keep his vow. Psalm 15:1,4 also speaks about this issue. *"Lord, who may abide in your tabernacle? Who may dwell in your holy hill? He who walks uprightly . . . who swears to his own hurt and does not change."* In other words, once he has made a covenant, an oath or a vow, he will not retract, even though it will be to his own hurt. One translation says, *"no matter how much it costs!"*

Covenants are made to keep—through the good times and the hard and tough times. That's why we make the covenant; we covenant to stick to our

80

vows through thick and thin! That's what marriage is all about it. It is covenant made before God, "*To have and to hold from this day forward, for better for worse; for richer for poorer; in sickness and in health; to love, to cherish, and to obey, till death us depart, according to God's holy ordinance, and thereto I pledge thee my troth.*" (Original wedding vows).

Do you find it hard to keep to your marriage vows? Let me encourage you with an irrevocable fact: the tide always comes in again! There are many times when the tide goes out in a marriage. You no longer feel loved. Your love wanes. You feel abused and rejected. You feel unappreciated. When the tide goes out in the ocean you see all the ugly things that have been swept up on the beach. In the same way you see all the ugly and detestable things in your husband. But, wait a minute. The tide always comes in again! It will happen. It is an eternal law. And when it does, the waves of God's love, forgiveness, and grace will cover all the ugly things and you will be glad that you waited, hung on, and were faithful to your vows.

We need to remind ourselves of the following Scriptures:

Deuteronomy 23:21, "*When you make a vow to the Lord your God, you shall not delay to pay it; for the Lord your God will surely require it of you, and it would be sin to you.*"

Ecclesiastes 5:4-5, "*When you make a vow to God, do not delay to pay it; for he has no pleasure in fools. Pay what you have vowed. It is better not to vow than to vow and not pay.*"

Prayer:
"*Oh God, help me to see the solemnity of my marriage vows. Help me to keep the covenant I have made with you and with my husband. Help me to be faithful and true, even when the going is tough. Thank you for your grace and your strength. Amen.*"

Affirmation:
I will keep covenant even through the dark and difficult times.

Day 39

God's Handmaiden

*"O turn unto me, and have mercy upon me; give thy strength unto thy
servant, and save the son of thy handmaid"*
(Psalm 86:16).

David is in a day of trouble. He is poor and needy. Violent men are after him. And as always, he cries to the Lord for help. David always turned to the Lord in his hour of need. He knew God as his Rock, his Fortress, his High Tower, and his Deliverer.

However, David says something very interesting in this plea for help. *"Save the son of thy handmaid,"* he cries to God. David, the king of all Israel was not ashamed to acknowledge his mother. The Scripture does not tell us her name but we see something of her character in David's prayer. David understood that God knew his mother. She was a godly woman. She was a bond slave of the Lord. The Hebrew word for "handmaid" is *amah* and means, "female servant, bondswoman." Do you notice that David doesn't say, "Jesse's handmaid," but "Thy handmaid"?

In essence, David is praying, "Lord, remember me. I am the son of my mother, your servant. Remember her daily and diligent prayers for me that are before your throne. Remember her dedication to you. Deliver me Lord, because of your bond slave."

I would love that testimony, wouldn't you? What a blessing if our children can cry out to God in their hour of need and say, "Lord, deliver me. I am the son (or daughter) of your bond slave. Her prayers are before your throne. You know her, Lord. Hear my cry because of the faithfulness of my mother."

David mentions his mother again in Psalm 116:16, *"O Lord, truly I am thy servant, I am thy servant, and the son of thy handmaid: thou hast loosed my bonds."* David freely confesses that he is a servant of the Lord. But even more, he openly acknowledges that he was born of a woman who is God's servant. It was not only David that freely expressed these words about his mother, but also God. The Holy Spirit, the inspirer of the Holy Scriptures, counted this worthy of being recorded.

As a bond slave of the Lord, David's mother birthed and raised a king of Israel. As a bond slave of the Lord, Mary was privileged to bring forth the King of kings and Lord of lords. In the face of shame, ridicule, and misunderstanding this humble born woman confessed, "*Behold the handmaid of the Lord; be it unto me according to thy word*" (Luke 1:38).

Do you notice that Mary was not a bond slave of anyone else but of the Lord? She was the "handmaiden of the Lord," ready and waiting to obey His command.

As you yield yourself as a bond slave to the Lord, open to His will and purposes for your life, who knows who will come forth from your womb to bless this world? You will not only birth them, but raise them to also become servants of the Lord.

Prayer:

"Oh God, it is my privilege to be your humble bond slave. Help me to be a faithful handmaid, always ready to obey your command. Oh Lord, please help me to live in such a way that my children will know that I have your ear in the courts of heaven. Help me to be faithful in prayer for my children. Amen."

Affirmation:

I am the handmaiden of the Lord, ready to do His bidding.

Day 40

Don't Give in to Doubt

*"Now the serpent was more subtle than any beast of the field which the Lord God had made. And he said unto the woman, Yea, **hath God said**, Ye shall not eat of every tree of the garden?"*
(Genesis 3:1).

The enemy of our souls is shrewd. He doesn't blatantly deceive us. He does it subtly. This was his first temptation to man and this is the way the deceiver of our souls continues to tempt us. He always starts by putting a doubt in our hearts. Am I really saved? Can God truly provide for me?

We must be careful to watch out for his doubts. He makes his temptation sound very plausible. In fact, verse 6 tell us that it will **sound good**, it will **feel pleasant**, it will **seem wise** and also cater to the **desire** of your soul.

Let's read the Scripture, "*When the woman saw that the tree was good for food, and that it was pleasant to the eyes, and a tree to be desired to make one wise . . .*" Satan always makes his temptations **seem** good and wise. In fact, it will often be very wise according to this world's ways, but God's Word is usually opposite to the way we feel and is totally opposite to the way of the world.

We see an example of this in our response to the first command that God ever gave to man. God's Word says, "*Be fruitful, and multiply, and replenish the earth.*" God is the author of life. He loves life. Satan, who comes to "*steal, kill and destroy*" is the destroyer of life and so he puts doubts in the hearts of God's people. "Does God really mean that? If you have one son and one daughter, you have done your part." And the doubtful questions keep coming.

It **seems wise** to delay your family or limit your family. You will have more time to fulfill your career or do things you have planned. You will have more money to build a better house, buy a better car and save for college education for your children. It **feels good** because you will have less work to do and you won't have to go through so many sleepless nights. It's **very desirable** because it will give you more time to do want you want in life. But, it is deception and it is contrary to God's Word.

It is amazing that the Christian church has imbibed this deception and now thinks that it is truth. Pre-marital counseling in most churches includes teaching on birth control! How incredibly Satan has imbedded his **deceptions** into the church!

Once Satan has sown the seed of doubt in our hearts, he then begins to **deliberately contradict** God's Word. We would not receive this contradiction if we didn't first have doubts about what God says. In verse 4, we read that the serpent said, *"Ye shall not surely die."* This was in total rebellion to God's direct word, *"Ye shall not eat of it, neither shall ye touch it, lest ye die."* We see how Satan works. First he starts with doubts, then it leads to disobedience, and we become totally deceived to the truth of God's Word.

The distortion of God's truth leads to the defecting of His commands, and then the degeneration and destruction of His designs.

I like to confess these words . . .

If Jesus said it, I'll believe it,
I'll believe it till I die!
It is written in the Bible,
His Word can never lie!
Though the mountains be removed
And cast into the sea,
If Jesus said it, I'll believe it,
I'll believe eternally!

Learn these lines and quote them out loud constantly. Teach them to your children, too.

Prayer:

"Dear Father, please help me to discern the doubts and deceptions the devil brings to my mind. Give me the courage to denounce them. Help me to be a woman of truth, not tossed to and fro, but standing strong in your Word. May my children see that I am not swayed by the philosophies of this world, but that I honor your Word no matter what the cost. Amen."

Affirmation:

The Word of God will keep me from sin or sin will keep me from the Word of God.

Day 41

Enough Hours in the Day?

"Sufficient unto the day is the evil thereof"
(Matthew 6:34).

Are you like me? I have so many visions, so many ideas, and so many things that I want to do but can never find the time to do them all. "If only I had more time! I need 48 hours in every day!" I would constantly sigh. But not anymore! I will no longer let these words pass my lips.

I was convicted about this recently when listening to a preacher who was also convicted of the same thing. He shared how he spoke similar words in the hearing of a dear old missionary who answered him, "Brother, God has given you 24 hours in every day. That's all you need!" Those words really spoke to me! If God wanted me to have more hours in the day, He would have provided more hours. What He has given is enough for each day. I work hard, but am now learning to be content with what I accomplish each day. It is never as much as I want, but it is enough in God's eyes.

Perhaps you find it hard to accomplish everything each day, too. Maybe you have been as frustrated as I have. Relax. Don't get upset over what you can't finish today. There's another day tomorrow. In the light of eternity, it's not going to matter whether you finish your task today or the next day.

Are you a home-educating mother? I know that often you find it hard to get through all the teaching you have planned for the day. Dear mother, God only expects you to accomplish what is possible in the hours He has given you. You don't have to get everything done. Be content with what you can accomplish. There is a new dawn tomorrow.

It is more important to set the right tone in your home and create an atmosphere of rest, peace, and harmony, than to make your children tense by getting through something just for the sake of getting through it. True teaching is not only making sure your child finishes a lesson, but making sure your child understands the lesson. One thing well learned is more effective than rushed lessons that are not understood, will be forgotten, or which are taught in a tense atmosphere. Do what you have time to do. That's all God expects.

There is no need to put expectations upon yourself or your children that God doesn't put upon you. Listen to these words from Psalm 103:14, "*He knows our frame; He remembers that we are dust.*" Isn't that comforting? God understands our frame because He created us. He created us with the ability to work for one day, not to put two days of work into one!

Of course, there is no excuse for laziness and negligence. It is most important to set goals and write your list for the day. Some mothers like to write their list the night before; others like to do it in the early morning quiet before the start the day. You will accomplish a lot more with a list. But remember, it's not the end of the world if you don't cross off everything on your list! I don't think that I have ever been able to accomplish everything on my list. Even if you cross off one or two things, you are accomplishing something.

When my children were little, sometimes I would only complete one extra task! Or, not even one! But, if I was faithful to mother my children and manage the home, that was all God required.

Psalm 90:12 says, *"So teach us to number our days, that we may apply our hearts unto wisdom."*

Prayer:

"I thank you, Father, that in your wisdom you have given us day and night for our blessing. You have given us the day to work and the night to rest. I thank you that you have given me the right number of hours for each day. Give me wisdom to use my days wisely. Help me to relax and not get upset when I can't do everything I planned. Amen."

Affirmation:

One day's trouble is enough for one day.

A Poem for You and Your Children to Learn:

Said the robin to the sparrow,
"I should really like to know,
Why these anxious human beings
Rush about and worry so."

Said the sparrow to the robin,
"Friend I think that it must be,
That they have no Heavenly Father,
Such as cares for you and me."

Don't Waste Your Brain Space

*"Casting **all** your care upon Him; for He careth for you"*
(1 Peter 5:7).

Isn't it amazing how we confess that we are believers, and yet we do not believe!

Do we believe God is caring for us? Do we believe God's Word in Psalm 139:17 that He is thinking about us all the time? In fact, His thoughts to us are more than the sands of the sea! If we believed this, we would not fret and worry all the time, would we? And yet, we seem to be professionals at worrying.

Many women spend most of their brain space worrying about this and that. What a waste! This space could be more profitably used to think positively. When we worry and think negatively, we do not help the situation. Worry makes the problem worse. Worry stifles creativity. You can't even see a way out of the problem when you worry. All you see is the problem.

Worry strangles the effectiveness of God's Word in your life and makes you unproductive. Matthew 13:22 tells us that *"the worries of this life"* choke the Word and we become unfruitful. In plain words, we cannot be fruitful when we worry!

The Amplified Version says, *"Casting the whole of your care—all your anxieties, all your worries, all your concerns, once and for all—on Him; for He cares for you affectionately, and cares about you watchfully."* God does not tell you to give some of your worries to Him. He tells you to give ALL your cares to Him. That means EVERY ONE. The big ones and the little ones. In fact, if you get into the habit of giving the little ones to Him, it will be natural to give the big ones to Him.

In Matthew 6:25-34, Jesus tells us not to worry about our life, what we should eat, what we should drink, what we should wear, or what will happen tomorrow! Dear mother, you don't have to waste brain space fretting about these things. Instead, thank Him that He has promised to provide them for you.

Worry is thinking about "me," rather than trusting God and His infallible Word. We waste a lot of valuable brain space thinking about ourselves. Many years ago, God spoke to me. His voice was so strong to my heart that it was like an audible voice. "Nancy," He said, "How can I reveal to you the needs of others if you are always thinking about yourself?" What a challenge!

If we spend all our brain space thinking about ourselves and insignificant things, we leave no room for God to bring to our mind the needs of others. Or, to give us creative dreams and visions. God wants to pour out His love upon His people and those who are poor and hurting, but He has to do it through us. He looks for those whose minds have space for Him to share His secrets, His strategies, and creative answers to the problems around us. Sadly, many times our minds are so consumed with self-pity and worry that God cannot get in even a fraction of an inch to tell us about someone who needs our prayers or help.

Will you throw all your worries upon the Lord, knowing that He is caring for you? He is thinking about you and knows the answers far better than you. Trust Him to work out your problems. Give Him room in your brain for the creative things He wants to say to you.

Prayer:

"Lord, I thank you that because you are thinking about me all the time, I don't have to waste my time thinking about myself. I trust you to care for me and for my family. I yield my mind to you for the important things you want to say to me. Amen."

Affirmation:

I am finished with fretting and regretting,
I am now receiving and believing!

Day 43

Family Togetherness

"When brother helps brother, theirs the strength of a fortress,
their cause is like a city gate barred, unassailable"
(Proverbs 18:19 Knox).

God created the family unit. It was His idea. It is how He planned for mankind to live—in a family! God wants families to be strong. Strong families make a strong nation.

Satan wants families to be weak. We must beware of allowing Satan to destroy our families. Let's face it; no family is perfect. We are trying to get along with a whole lot of sinners. Because of this, every one of us can face hurts and grievances in our immediate and extended families. Family members can often do something that hurts us or say words that pierce like a sword. Unless we walk in the spirit, it is easy to allow unforgiveness and hurt to fester in family relationships.

We cannot allow this to happen. We must be big enough to lay down our own agenda. We must say No to the flesh and allow the Holy Spirit to work in our lives. We must show grace. We need to forgive. We may have to forgive again and again and again. Seventy times seven! This is God's way and the only way that works.

Seek to strengthen your family—and your extended family of aunts, uncles and cousins. A strong extended family is a powerful force in the nation. Here is a little acrostic about Family Togetherness.

T Traveling through life is no good on your own,
To do it with family is the best way known.

O Old and young, the toddlers and teens,
All add to the mix with their family genes.

G Gathering together as much as we can,
Putting aside time to be with the clan.

E Enjoying suppers, parties, and feasts
Where we all bring food and special treats.

T Talking and laughing, shouting, debating,
    It's a great lot of fun, certainly not sedating!

H Helping one another in times of need,
    Going the extra mile to do the deed.

E Embracing the children, the more the merrier,
    Enlarging our homes to all fit in one area.

R Remembering each other, even those far away,
    Cementing the bonds by praying each day.

N Never holding a grudge—for hurt or lies,
    Forgiving freely when offences arise.

E Expect perfection? We all fall on our face,
    We're sinners redeemed, needing God's grace.

S Strengthened by unity—we must guard it well,
    And watch "little foxes" don't come in to dwell.

S Serving each other with a humble mind,
    This is the way as a family we'll bind.

Prayer:

"Father, please help me to do my part to strengthen my extended family. Help me to overlook and forgive offences. Help me to love in the face of hatred. Give me grace to forgive even when it seems too hard to forgive. Thank you, Lord, for your power enabling me to do this because this is your perfect will. Amen."

Affirmation:

I am a family strengthener!

Day 44

Feminine Power

Part 1

*"And to Adam he said, Because you have listened to the voice of your wife,
and have eaten of the tree of which I commanded you, 'You shall not eat of it,'
cursed is the ground because of you"*
(Genesis 3:17 RSV).

I wonder if you are aware of the influence you wield over your husband—for good or for bad. We have feminine power and charms that can subtly turn the hearts of our men.

Satan knows this and he makes the most of it! He used this knowledge to tempt the man in the very beginning. Satan knew that if he was to tempt Adam first, that Adam would have stood up for truth and told the serpent to get off! It was a different matter with Eve. She was more easily persuaded, but more than that, the serpent knew that she had the power to sway her husband.

Basically, men want to please their wives. They want to make them happy, because that makes them happy. Just as women have a weakness to deception; men have a tendency to be influenced by their wives. This may not be obvious in their initial reactions and response to what we say, but in the end, our words and influence can determine their behavior and course of action. We can build up our marriage or we can destroy it. We hold this power in our hands. No wonder Proverbs 14:1 says, *"Every wise woman builds her house, but the foolish pulls it down with her hands."*

We see the influence of women throughout history. Through Marxist, feministic, and humanistic thinking, Satan duped the minds of millions of women to turn away from their home and God's original plan for marriage and motherhood.

But, that is only the beginning. He used them to seduce the men. We now have an epidemic of wimpiness—men who are afraid to lead their families in the ways of God; men who do not take up their responsibility to provide for their family; men who hand over the teaching and guidance of their children to the government or even the church. They have forgotten that they are patriarchs with the anointing to build a godly dynasty and take dominion for God. This has come about through the subtle influence of women.

Even King Solomon, the wisest man who ever lived, turned from the living God to serve idols because of the influence of his wives. We read about this in 1 Kings 11:1-11, *"But King Solomon loved many foreign women, as well as the daughter of Pharaoh (gave his heart to them): women from the nations of whom the Lord had said to the children of Israel, 'You shall not intermarry with them, nor they with you. For surely they will turn away your hearts after their gods.' Solomon clung to them in love . . . For it was so, when Solomon was old that his wives turned his heart after other gods; and his heart was not loyal to the Lord his God, as was the heart of his father David . . . Then Solomon built a high place for Chemosh the abomination of Moab and for Moloch the abomination of the people of Ammon. And he did likewise for all his foreign wives, who burned incense and sacrificed to their gods. So the Lord became angry with Solomon . . ."*

Women were Solomon's weakness. He was a strong man, the leader of a nation; a wise man to whom people came from nations round about to receive wisdom; a man of vision and order, of whom the Queen of Sheba exclaimed, *"the half has not been told!"* And yet he was influenced for evil by women! I am sure it did not happen overnight, but their continual subtle wiles wore him down until in the end, instead of pleasing God, he pleased his wives and made shrines for them to serve their foreign gods! We can cite many more examples. Samson was duped by Delilah. King Ahab became a wimp by seeking to please his wife Jezebel.

No man is exempt from the influence of a woman! I find this scary! I am aware of my own influence as a wife. I am guilty of having influenced my husband negatively instead of in a righteous way. I find that I must walk in the fear of the Lord and be continually aware of my feminine, but powerful influence. Our influence is not only in the big things of life, but the little daily things. By our attitude and the words we speak we have the power to affect our husband's attitude to life, his home and family, his work, and the people in his life.

If we speak degrading and negative words to him personally, he will never rise to be the man God intends him to be. As a woman we have power to make great men or little men.

In the same way, we influence our children, and ultimately the whole of society. In most cases, after each new king of Israel or Judah is introduced to us in the Bible, it gives the name of his mother and then immediately states whether her son did *"that which was evil in the sight of the Lord"* or whether he did *"that which was right in the sight of the Lord."* The influence of his mother not only determined the future of her son, but the outcome of the whole nation!

Prayer:

"Father, please help me to be aware of the feminine power you have given to me as a woman. Help me to influence my husband and children to righteousness, to love, to joy, and to positivity. Save me from being a negative influence. Amen."

Affirmation:

I am a society changer!

Day 45

Feminine Power

Part 2

"And the Lord God said, It is not good that man should be alone:
I will make him a help meet for him"
(Genesis 2:18).

God created women with enticing charms that can sway the hearts and thinking of men. He did not give us this power to use negatively, but positively.

God created us to be a helper to our husband. We are to make his life great. He can't do without us. God said that it was not good for man to be alone. He cannot survive without a helper! If we think that we can just look after ourselves, we miss out on the purpose for which God created us. If we think we have the freedom to influence our husband to do what we want him to do, we are on the wrong track. If we think we can say what we like and put our husband down with negative words, we are at cross purposes with God!

Let's get it straight. We were created to help him in the great task God has given to both of us to be fruitful, multiply, replenish the earth, subdue, and take dominion for God in this world (Genesis 1:28). We have been given a powerful mandate. There is no room for pulling down or leading our husband on a deviant path. To fulfill this world-encompassing Genesis command we cannot be anything else than positive, uplifting, encouraging supporters!

God uses the words "help meet" to describe his purpose for us. The word "meet" is the Hebrew word *neged* and means "part opposite, counterpart, mate, in front of." In other words, she is opposite to man, but fits him perfectly like a glove.

The word "help" is the Hebrew word *ezer* which means "helper, to come to the aid of." The amazing thing is that it is the same Hebrew word that is used when it speaks of God being our helper! Here are a few examples:

*"God is our **help** and shield"* (Psalm 33:20).

*"O God, thou art my **help** and my deliverer"* (Psalm 70:5).

*"Our **help** is in the name of the Lord, who made heaven and earth"* (Psalm 124:8).

How wonderful to have God for our help. He is always available to help us when we cry out to Him. Am I the same kind of help to my husband? Am I always available to help him? The psalmist proclaims, ***"Happy** is he that has the*

95

God of Jacob for his help" (Psalm 146:5). If we walk according to God's plan, we will have a happy husband! What about your husband? Does he confess, "My wife makes me a happy man!"

Even more amazing is that this word *ezer* is **first used** regarding a wife, before it is used regarding God! In "the law of the first mention" the word *help* is given to a wife! This puts much importance on this issue. We reveal the image of God when we help our husband.

How Can I help my husband?
I help him by coming alongside to help him as he needs me.
I help him by speaking sweetly, kindly, and positively into his life.
I help him by fulfilling the role that God has given to me rather than competing for his role of provider and leader of the home. I don't help my husband by taking his responsibility. It undermines his manhood.
I help him by caring for our children and making our home a place of joy and sweetness.
I help him by making life easier for him to do his work.
I help him by being a sounding board for his dreams and visions for life.
I help him by caring for him physically and nutritionally.
I help him by having an aroma-filled, nutritious meal ready for him when he returns to home at the end of the day. This is one task of your great motherhood career that you cannot let slip! It is more important than you realize!
I help him by having the home ready for him when he arrives home—toys and mess cleaned up and thrown out of sight!
I help him by being excited to see him when he arrives—even if I have had a lousy day! It is a strong woman who can put aside her self-pitying spirit and by faith put on a smiling face. Greet your husband with joy and talk about the troubles later on—after the evening meal and the children are in bed.
I help him by being available to him sexually. I was created to be "one flesh" with my husband, to delight him rather than deprive him.

Prayer:
"Father, please help me to fulfill the purpose for which you created me. Help me to use my feminine influence to support my husband in the work you have given him to do. Please teach me how to help my husband just as you come to my aid to help me. Amen."

Affirmation:
I am my husband's happy helper!

Day 46

Feminine Power

Part 3

"But let it be the hidden man of the heart, in that which is not corruptible, even the ornament of a meek and quiet spirit, which is in the sight of God of great price"
(1 Peter 3:4).

There is another word that is used regarding God that is also **first used** about a wife. This time it is Sarah. Genesis 12:14-15 says, *"So it was, when Abram came into Egypt, that the Egyptians saw the woman, that she was very beautiful. The princes of Pharaoh also saw here and **commended** her to Pharaoh. And the woman was taken to Pharaoh's house."*

The word "commended" in the Hebrew is *hallel* which means "praise" and is nearly always used for praising God! It is where we get the word, Hallelujah! Here it is used to praise a woman, and it is the first mention of "praise" in the Bible! Do you like that?

The Bible tells us that Sarah was a "great beauty," but it is obvious that her beauty was more than physical. She was radiant with inner beauty. It was the unfading beauty of a gentle and quiet spirit (1 Peter 3:4 NIV). This inner beauty and poise kept the courtiers from using Sarah themselves and instead they sang her praises to Pharaoh.

The Talk of the Town

There is another passage which uses *hallel* to praise a woman. In fact, it uses it three times! I am sure you'll guess that it is in Proverbs 31:28-31, *"Her children rise up and called her blessed; her husband also and he **praises** her: Many daughters have done well, but you excel them all. Charm is deceitful and beauty is vain, but a woman who fears the Lord, she shall be **praised**. Give her of the fruit of her hands, and let her own works **praise** her in the gates."*

This virtuous woman is faithful to her husband. He can faithfully trust in her. She is committed to the building of her home. She is not jealous of her husband being an elder in the city gates, for she has the responsibility to guard her home gates, which she does judiciously. She is a hard worker. This woman is praised by her husband, praised by her children, and praised by the men in the city gates! She is the talk of the town!

You couldn't get more honor than that, could you?

Prayer:

"Father, help me to remember that I am not a separate entity to my husband, but you created us to be 'one flesh.'"

Affirmation:

I am my husband's delighter.

Day 47

The "Filled" Word

Part 1

*"O Lord, how manifold are thy works! In wisdom hast thou made them all:
the earth is **full of thy riches**"*
(Psalm 104:2).

Filled." It doesn't sound such a bad word, does it? I wonder why so many people hate it. It's strange that so many Christians hate it when God loves it! In fact, this word describes who God is. He fills the heavens and the earth. He fills all in all—and Jesus is the fullness of Him who fills all in all. The whole earth is full of His glory. He is filled with majesty, filled with righteousness, and filled with compassion. He does not have these attributes in a little measure. but is filled with them.

God does not take long to introduce this word to us. He uses it in the very first chapter of the Bible.

Genesis 1:28 says, *"And God blessed them, and God said to them, 'Be fruitful and multiply, and fill the earth and subdue it' . . ."* It is interesting that the very first words that God spoke to man included the word *fill*. It is obviously very much a part of God's heart. He loves abundance.

After God destroyed mankind through the flood (apart from Noah and his family), He repeated the same command again. This time He repeated it twice. First in Genesis 9:1 and again in v. 7, *"And God blessed Noah and his sons, and said to them, 'Be fruitful and multiply, and **fill** the earth' . . ."*

The Hebrew word is *male* which means to "fill to overflowing." Many take objection to this command today. They certainly don't want to fill their families to overflowing. They would rather fill their homes with "stuff"—more gadgets, more furniture, bigger TVs and computers, etc. Yet, it seems that every time God speaks about children, He uses this despised word.

When Jacob and his family went down to Egypt there were only 70 of them. Four hundred years later they emerged a mighty nation. Exodus 1:7 says, *"The children of Israel were fruitful, and increased abundantly, and multiplied, and waxed exceeding mighty; and the land was **filled** with them."* They became *"more and mightier"* than the Egyptians who began to fear them. Their fear turned to persecuting the Hebrews and making them slaves. But, the more the Egyptians afflicted them the more they multiplied. This is God's purpose for His people.

He wants them to fill the earth with His glory—His love, peace, truth, and salvation.

Not only did the children of Israel fill the land of Egypt, but when God brought them into the Promised Land they filled that land also. Talking about the Israelites Psalm 80:8-11 says, *"Thou hast brought a vine out of Egypt: thou hast cast out the heathen, and planted it. Thou preparedst room before it, and didst cause it to take deep root, and it **filled** the land. The hills were covered with the shadow of it, and the boughs thereof were like the goodly cedars. She sent out her boughs unto the sea, and her branches unto the river."* God's intention is always for His people to fill the land.

We know that because of their rebellion and sin God eventually had to cast His people out of their land. However, He will never give up on the His promised land for His people and has given us hundreds of promises of how He will bring them back again. Ezekiel 36:37-38 is just one of hundreds of these promises where it says, *"I will increase them with men like a flock. As the holy flock, as the flock of Jerusalem in her solemn feasts; so shall the waste cities be **filled** with flocks of men: and they shall know that I am the Lord."* The waste cities are already being filled again and will be filled more and more. God is going to fill His land with His people.

Numbers 14:21 says, *"But as truly as I live, all the earth shall be **filled** with the glory of the Lord."* This is not talking about creation, but God's people who bear His image in the earth. God wants this earth to be filled with His image. God wants His land to be *"**filled** with flocks of men"* (Ezekiel 36:38 and Psalm 80:8-9). He wants Israel to *"**fill** the face of the world"* (Isaiah 27:6).

God's picture of a blessed family is one filled with children. Society is brainwashed to think differently than God thinks and many think they know better than God. But what does He say? *"As arrows are in the hand of a mighty man; so are children of the youth. Happy is the man that has his quiver **full** of them: they shall not be ashamed, but they shall speak with the enemies in the gate"* (Psalm 127:4-5).

The parents who have their quiver full are happy! Actually, the Hebrew word in this Scripture is a double word which should be translated, "happy, happy." The parents who have their quiver full are not ashamed. The parents who have their quiver full will have children who know how to speak against the evil practices in the land, even in high places. The gate in Bible days was the civic center of the town, the place of administration of justice.

What about the allegory of motherhood God presents to us in Ezekiel 19:10-14? The mother in this passage is pictured as *"fruitful and **full** of branches."* The branches speak of the children coming forth from a godly union. The mother is not pictured as a spindly tree with only one or two branches. No, she is full of branches, which is what is expected of a healthy tree.

Zechariah 8:4-5 is one of my favorite Scriptures. It is a picture of what Jerusalem will be like when God dwells there. *"Thus saith the Lord of hosts: There shall yet old men and old women dwell in the streets of Jerusalem, and every man with his staff in his hand for very age. And the streets of the city shall be **full** of boys and girls playing in the streets thereof."* What a beautiful picture of children playing while the old people walk the city streets with their canes and watch the children in the city squares. Did you notice that there are more than a few children playing? The streets are filled with boys and girls. How God delights to see them playing together.

Here's one more Scripture. Luke 14:23 says, *"Go out into the highways and hedges, and compel them to come in, that my house may be **filled**."* God loves to have a full house. It's part of His character. If we have God's heart, we'll want to have a full house too.

Prayer:

"Dear Father, I pray that you will change my heart. Save me from thinking miserly, but help me to think like you think. Help me to have a 'filled' mentality. Amen."

Affirmation:

I'm filling up my home with God's blessings.

Keep on Being Filled

Part 2

"Be filled with the Spirit; speaking to yourselves in psalms and hymns and spiritual songs, singing and making melody in your heart to the Lord; giving thanks always for all things unto God and the Father in the name of our Lord Jesus Christ"
(Ephesians 5:18-20).

We are learning that God loves the word *filled*. It is very much a part of His vocabulary. He doesn't want us to be half-filled, but filled to the top and spilling over. He wants us to burst at the seams. Let's look at some other ways God wants us to be filled.

God wants us to be filled with the Holy Spirit

In Ephesians 5:18 the word "filled" is the Greek word *pleroo* which means "to fill up, to cause to abound, to supply liberally, to flood, and to diffuse throughout." The verb is in the present imperative tense which means that it is something that should happen continually. The full meaning is to be "constantly, moment by moment controlled by the Holy Spirit."

It is so easy to run dry, isn't it? We can start the day asking the Lord to fill us with His Holy Spirit but somehow the challenges and frustrations of the day drain us out. We need to continually ask the Holy Spirit to fill us—to control our thoughts, attitudes, and actions. When you are drained, ask Him to flood your mind and heart again. It doesn't matter how many times you come to Him to be filled. God's well is inexhaustible and it never runs dry. Keep being filled to overflowing so you can bless your family. If you are only half-filled, you have nothing to give to others.

God wants us to be filled with joy and peace

Romans 15:13 says, *"Now the God of hope fill you with all joy and peace in believing, that ye may abound in hope, through the power of the Holy Ghost."*

God does not want us to have half peace and half nervous tension. He wants us to be *filled* with peace. Peace is not controlled by what happens in our lives but by the power of the Holy Spirit controlling us. Many things, little and big, constantly happen to disturb our peace. But you don't have to let them disturb you. When something happens that upsets you, look to the Lord, instead of the problem.

God has promised to keep you in perfect peace as you keep your heart and mind fixed on Him. The word "peace" in Isaiah 26:3-4 is a double word in the Hebrew. It should be translated "peace, peace." This promise is reiterated again in Philippians 4:6-7. God says that He will keep us in *peace that passes all understanding"* when we stop worrying and instead turn our hearts to Him.

But, there is also joy. Joy and peace are twins. When our hearts are filled with peace, we will be filled with joy. When the people of Antioch persecuted Paul and Barnabas and expelled them out of their city, they didn't despair. Instead, they were *"filled with joy, and with the Holy Ghost"* (Acts 13:52).

What about when people hate you, say you are evil, persecute you, and speak about you because of your beliefs? Are you full of indignation and self-pity? That's how we naturally feel, isn't it? But Jesus tells us not to worry, but to, *"Rejoice ye in that day, and leap for joy; for, behold, your reward is great in heaven"* (Luke 6: 23). Leaping for joy sounds like being *filled* with joy, doesn't it? Have you ever tried it?

I think the secret is living in the presence of the Lord for *"In thy presence is fullness of joy"* (Psalm 16:11). Read these wonderful Scriptures too: John 15:11; Acts 2:28; 2 Corinthians 7:4; 1 Peter 1:8 and 1 John 1:4.

God wants us to be filled with righteousness

Philippians 1:11 tells us that we are to be *"filled with the fruits of righteousness, which are by Jesus Christ."* Our righteousness is only by Jesus Christ. We have none of our own. Christ lives in us by His Holy Spirit, but we must let Him fill our lives. As Christ Jesus, and His Word, fill our minds and lives, we will be filled with His righteousness (Matthew 5:6).

Prayer:

"Blessed Father, I don't want to be half-filled. Please keep filling me with your Holy Spirit so I will be filled to the top and flowing over. Amen."

Affirmation:

I want to be an overflowing vessel.

Day 49

Keep on Being Filled

Part 3

According to thy name, O God, so is thy praise unto the ends of the earth:
*thy right hand is **full** of righteousness"*
(Psalm 48:10).

We continue to discover how much God wants our lives to be filled. He is not a half-filled God but a God of fullness and He wants us to be the same.

God wants us to be filled with praise

Psalm 71:8 says, *"Let my mouth be **filled** with thy praise and with thy honor all the day."* Remember we are talking about the word *filled*. It is not enough to praise the Lord now and then when things are going great. Praise should fill our mouths so that it spills over in every circumstance. Even the frustrating ones!

I was recently reading a book about a missionary in Belize. Someone who was mad at her came and destroyed her beautiful flower beds—they ripped out all the plants, broke the rose bushes, and threw them on the path. When she found this mess, instead of getting mad, she started saying, "Praise the Lord, Praise the Lord, Praise the Lord . . ."

"What are you doing?" a friend asked. She explained that she had read about saying "Praise the Lord" ten times before you say anything else when something traumatic happens or upsets you.

"Does it help?" the friend asked.

"At least it gives me time to reflect that for some reason God allowed this to happen to me," she replied.

This might be something you could try, too.

God wants us to be filled with laughter

Job 8:20-21 says, *"Behold, God will not cast away a perfect man, neither will he help the evil doers: Till he **fill** thy mouth with laughing, and thy lips with rejoicing"* (Psalm 126:1-2).

We've all heard the phrase, "Laughter is the best medicine." It is not an old wives' tale. It is proven medically. Laughing protects the heart, relaxes the body, relieves stress, releases endorphins, and boosts the immune system which improves resistance to disease. It sounds like we could do with a dose of laughing, doesn't it? My mother told me about a man she read about who was diagnosed with cancer. He decided that if he only had three weeks to live, he might as well die happy. He asked people to bring him all the funny movies they could find. He laughed so much that he laughed himself back to health!

Sometimes life is so challenging that it is hard to find something to laugh about, isn't it? But we need to look for it. Laugh at everything you can. Laugh when the children do funny things, even when it messes the house. Laugh together with your husband. Most of all, laugh at yourself. When you hear laughter, join in. Laughing is contagious—more than coughs and colds. I remember reading a book as I flew on the plane between Los Angeles and New Zealand. Some incidents were so funny that I couldn't stop laughing out loud. People around me started to laugh too, even though they didn't know what I was laughing about.

We know the adage, "An apple a day keeps the doctor away" but recently I read that "A laugh a day will keep the heart attack away." My brother often says that people could get more refreshed laughing at some funny stories at church than listening to another sermon!

Start with smiling. Smiling is the prerequisite to laughter. The more you smile, just for the fun of smiling, the more apt you will be to laugh. Smile at your husband, smile at your children, smile at the joy of being a mother in your home, smile at the birds and butterflies flying by, and smile because you are alive. The smile is the first thing we look for in our newborn baby—and then to hear their belly laugh. What contagious laughter.

Let's be filled with smiles and laughter. Let laughter ring throughout every room of your home.

Prayer:

"Fill Thou my life, O Lord my God,
In every part with praise,
That my whole being may proclaim
Thy being and Thy ways" Amen.
~ Horatius Bonar

Affirmation:

I choose to praise instead of to grumble!

Day 50

Keep on Being Filled

Part 4

"And to know the love of Christ, which passeth knowledge,
*that ye might be **filled** with all the **fullness** of God"*
(Ephesians 3:19).

Every attribute of God He has in fullness. And Jesus is the fullness of God who fills all in all. He also wants His creatures, created in His image to walk in His fullness. Read these wonderful Scriptures: Ephesians 1:23; 3:19; 4:10, 13 and Colossians 1:19 and 2:9.

God wants us to be filled with faith

Stephen and Barnabas were both filled with faith and the Holy Spirit (Acts 6:5, 8, 15; and 11:24). How I need the Holy Spirit to fill me with faith. Sometimes I find that I am filled with unbelief. But that is the opposite to the life of Christ who lives within me. That proves I am living in the flesh and not in the spirit. When I live in the spirit I can trust God to work out His plan, even when everything looks the opposite.

God wants us to be filled with wisdom, understanding, and knowledge

Paul prayed for the Colossian believers, *"that ye might be **filled** with the knowledge of his will in all wisdom and spiritual understanding; that ye might walk worthy of the Lord unto all pleasing, being fruitful in every good work, and increasing in the knowledge of God"* (Colossians 1:9-10; 2:2). Pray this prayer for yourself. Pray it for your children.

It is through God's wisdom and understanding that we fill our home with riches—not the so-called riches of material possessions—but the riches of the warmth of His love, peace, joy, security, and the bond of family commitment. Proverbs 24:3-4 says, *"Through wisdom is a house builded; and by understanding it is established; and by knowledge shall the chambers be **filled** with all precious and pleasant riches."* Precious and pleasant! What lovely adjectives to describe a home. I can't think of anything more wonderful than filling our home with these riches.

God wants us to be filled with light

Matthew 6:22 says, *"The light of the body is the eye: if therefore thine eye be single, thy whole body shall be full of light"* (Luke 11:33-36). Even a little bit of darkness of sin fades the light. Jesus, who is the light of the world, lives in us, and He wants His light to fill us and shine through us. This is why it is important to come before the Lord daily to let Him expose any darkness that has crept into our lives—the darkness of disobedience, deception, deceit, doubt, discord, discontent, despair, despondency and defeat. As we confess these sins and renounce them, God's light can fill our lives again.

God wants us to be filled with good works

Do you remember the story of Dorcas who was raised from the dead? You can read about her in Acts 9:36-42. She was a woman who was *"full of good works and almsdeeds which she did."* She cared for the poor and made clothes and coats for the widows.

Ephesians 2:10 says that we have been *"created in Christ Jesus unto good works, which God hath before ordained that we should walk in them."* We are not saved by our good works, but we are saved to do good works.

One of the greatest works that we can do is to embrace motherhood. 1 Timothy 5:10 talks about a woman who is *"well reported of for good works."* The Scripture goes on to list her good works—the first being motherhood! Isn't this interesting? It is the first good work that is mentioned.

When you have all your little children around, you may not have time to do many other good works, such as sewing for the poor and feeding the hungry. But God says that you are doing the most important work when you embrace motherhood and train and teach your children well. Dear mother, give it all you have. Don't mother half-heartedly. Walk in the **fullness** of motherhood. Be filled to overflowing with the anointing of motherhood as you nurture you children each day.

As your children grow and you have more time, you can move on to many other good works, which will all be an extension of your motherhood. You can read about the rest of the good works in 1 Timothy 5:10.

Prayer:

"Father, thank you for reminding me that motherhood is the first good work that I am to do. Help me to do it fully and not half-heartedly. Amen."

Affirmation:

I am doing a great work as I prepare my children to influence the world for God.

Keep on Being Filled

Part 5

*"Till we all come in the unity of the faith, and of the knowledge of the Son of God, unto a perfect man, unto the measure of the stature of the **fullness** of Christ"*
(Ephesians 4:13).

How much more does God want us to be filled? There's still more.

God wants us to be filled with grace and truth

John 1:14-16 says, *"And the Word was made flesh, and dwelt among us, (and we beheld his glory, the glory as of the only begotten of the Father,) **full** of grace and truth . . . And of his **fullness** have we all received, and grace for grace."* Jesus was full of grace and truth. But the amazing truth is that we have received of His fullness. Because Jesus lives in us by His Holy Spirit, we too, can be full of grace and truth.

Jesus never compromised truth, but He ministered it with grace. There are many who do not believe or understand God's truth. We must not hold back speaking the truth to them, but we must share it with love and compassion, remembering that we too were once deceived and are still learning each day.

God wants us to be filled with mercy

God's wisdom is filled with mercy (James 3:17). God Himself is full of mercy and He wants us to be the same. We have so many opportunities to show mercy in word and deed each day. May we overflow with this grace.

God wants us to have full assurance of faith

Hebrews 10:22 says, *"Let us draw near with a true heart in **full assurance** of faith, having our hearts sprinkled from an evil conscience, and our bodies washed with pure water."*

Have you done things in your past that make you feel unclean? You feel that you are not worthy? Do not undermine the power of the cross of Jesus Christ. When Jesus died, He did not die in vain. He died to completely free you from the guilt of your sin. When you come to Him in contrition and repentance and confess your sins, He promises to forgive you, cleanse you, and make you clean. When you have been cleansed by the blood of Jesus, you are totally cleansed. God sees the blood of His beloved Son and no longer sees your sin. This is what God does:

He cleanses and forgives you totally
There is no sin that is too hard for God to forgive. The death of Jesus was not in vain. Read 1 John 1:7, 9 and Hebrews 7:25.

He never remembers your sin again
It is buried under the blood of Jesus. Read Hebrews 8:12.

He removes your sins as far as the east is from the west
Read Psalm 103:12. Once a year Aaron, the High Priest, picked two goats for sacrifice. One was to be a sin offering. This goat was slaughtered and the blood was taken into the Holy of Holies. After this he laid his hands on the other goat's head and confessed over it all the sins and rebellion of the Israelites. They chose a man to take this goat, carrying all the people's sins upon it, into a desolate land. It was called the scapegoat. It reminds us how our sins are taken away, never to be recovered again. I have a picture of the scapegoat on my computer screen as a reminder of this wonderful truth. You can read about it in Leviticus 16.

He blots out your sins like a thick cloud blots out the sun
Read Isaiah 43:25 and 44:22.

You can come into God's throne room with full assurance of faith.

Prayer:
"Lord Jesus, I thank you that your death upon the cross and your precious blood you shed is effective to cleanse me from all my sin. I thank you that I am cleansed and can come into your presence with full assurance. Amen."

Affirmation:
I'm tired of being half-filled; I want to be filled to overflowing.

Day 52

Keep Being Filled

Part 6

*"The earth shall be **full** of the knowledge of the Lord,*
as the waters cover the sea"
(Isaiah 11:9).

I am sure you are getting the message that God wants us to be filled to over-flowing with His life and love. May He save us from living half-hearted and half-filled lives.

God wants us to be filled with good food

Deuteronomy 11:14-15 says, *"I will give you the rain of your land in his due season . . . that thou mayest gather in thy corn, and thy wine, and thine oil . . . that thou mayest eat and be **full**."* God doesn't want anyone left out. In Deuteronomy 26:12 He speaks about *"the Levite, the stranger, the fatherless, and the widow, that they may eat within thy gates, and be **filled**."*

When God talks about eating, He talks about eating to the full! Do you like that? The blessing of the Lord is to be filled! God wants to not only fill us with spiritual blessings, but physical blessings also. This is the nature of God, not to leave us half-filled, but overflowing and satisfied.

We also have the same instinct. We want our children are filled. When visitors come, we make sure they have plenty to eat and are filled. It is against the nature of God to be stingy with food. He fills us to overflowing.

When Jesus fed the multitudes, He made sure they were filled, and with food left over, too (Matthew 14:20 and 15:37)!

Proverbs 23:6-7 NLT says, *"Don't eat with people who are stingy; don't desire their delicacies. 'Eat and drink,' they say, but they don't mean it. They are always thinking about how much it costs."* Enjoy filling your children's tummies. It is God-like! But make sure it is with **good** food, not junk! Read Psalm 23:2, 5 and Ezekiel 34:14-15 to see how God loves to fill us with good food.

God wants our homes to be filled with His glory

God filled His house on earth with His glory. He came in His glory when they praised and worshipped the Lord (2 Chronicles 5:13-14). He wants our homes to be filled with the glory of His presence, too. It is a big task to keep our homes filled with God's presence. There are so many things that come to quench His presence. We have to be on guard to deal with these issues and keep our homes free from these negative influences. Read the following Scriptures: Deuteronomy 7:26; Ephesians 4:30-31 and 1 Thessalonians 5:19.

God wants us to have a full reward

God encourages us to be diligent and hold on to what we have in Christ and what we have gained in our walk with God. He doesn't want us to get a half reward but a full reward. He doesn't want us to miss out on all that He has planned for us.

2 John 8 says, *"Look to yourselves, that we lose not those things which we have wrought, but that we receive a full reward."* Read also Hebrews 6:11.

God wants us to be filled with the blessing of the Gospel

Romans 15:29 says, *"I shall come in the **fullness** of the blessing of the gospel of Christ."* We should be filled with the fullness of the blessing of the gospel, so much so, that we are ready to share the truth of the gospel to everyone we meet. It should be an overflowing of the fullness of Christ in us. We must not hold it back to only share with those who we know will accept it. We must be ready to share God's truth with everyone with whom we come in contact. In season and out of season. We must be ready to challenge every idea that does not bow to the Lordship of Christ.

May you be filled to overflowing each new day.

Prayer:

"Father, please fill me again with your Holy Spirit. Fill my home with your holy presence. Reveal to me anything that is grieving the Holy Spirit in my home. Amen."

Affirmation:

I'm filling my home with everything that pleases the Lord and throwing out everything that displeases Him.

Further Study:

Go to page 219.

Day 53

Follow the Leader

*"The sheep hear his voice: and he calleth his own sheep by name,
and leadeth them out . . . he goeth before them, and the sheep follow him:
for they know his voice"*
(John 10:3-4).

Jesus is the great Shepherd of the sheep. He is the One who shows us how to be shepherdesses of our little flocks.

I was born and bred in the land of New Zealand, down at the bottom of the world. New Zealand is a sheep country and my father was a world champion sheep shearer. In New Zealand, the sheep farmers do not have a little flock of sheep like the Eastern shepherd. They have thousands of sheep. When bringing the sheep in from the paddocks for drenching, crutching, or shearing, the shepherds drive the sheep. They do this, riding on their horses and with the help of trained barking dogs called Hunterways. My father was an expert trainer of these dogs.

However, the Eastern shepherd to whom Jesus is likened does not drive his sheep. He walks in front of them and leads the way. He watches out for the pitfalls. He faces the danger first in order to protect his sheep. When visiting Israel, I loved to watch the Bedouin shepherd leading his little flock of sheep and goats across the desert.

As a mother shepherdess, we must not drive our children. It only leads to rebellion and defiance. We walk in front of them and lead the way. Jesus beckoned each of his disciples to, *"Come, follow me."* In the same way, we tell our children, "Come, children, follow me. I'll show you the way to go. I'll lead you on the right path. You won't stumble if you follow me" (Jeremiah 31:9). We give them vision. Inspire them to greatness. Motivate them to godliness. Encourage them to dream great dreams. Stir them to fulfill their destiny which has been marked out for them before the foundation of the world.

I am always challenged by the Scripture in Ezekiel 16:44, *"As is the mother, so is her daughter."* As we walk out in front of our children, what kind of an example are we giving them? Are we happy for them to follow in our footsteps?

The good shepherdess also leads her flock to still waters. She makes her home a place of peace. I know this is not an easy task, especially if you are raising a large family. Children are not perfect (nor are we) and there are often storms to quiet. The good shepherdess not only protects her children from the

112

storms outside, but seeks God's wisdom to quell the storms inside the home. Read Psalm 23:3 and Isaiah 49:10.

We are to also lead our flock in the paths of righteousness. Did you notice that it says to **lead** them? Our children will watch what we do and follow in our paths. They notice whether our walk with the Lord is genuine or hypocritical. They notice if we take them to church on Sundays but do not live like a believer throughout the week. They notice whether we love to pray. They notice whether we love to read God's Word or rarely pick it up from day to day. They notice if we watch movies that we wouldn't want them to see. Do we have one standard for our children and another for ourselves?

Remember, we are out in front showing them the way. May we be like the great Shepherd, *"Who teaches you to profit, who leads you by the way you should go"* (Isaiah 48:17).

Prayer:

"Lord, please help me to shepherd my little flock like you shepherd me. Help me to be a good example for them to follow. Amen."

Affirmation:

I am walking out in front of my children, inspiring them to godly living.

Day 54

Free to Be You!

"The Lord looks from heaven; He sees all the sons of men.
From the place of his habitation He looks on all the inhabitants of the earth;
He fashions their hearts individually; He considers all their works"
(Psalm 33:13-15).

How amazing that God individually fashions each new inhabitant of the earth. There is not one who is the same. Not only does this cause us to worship our awesome and creative God but it also liberates us to be the special person God created us to be.

I am different to everyone else in the world. I am free from the bondages of having to be like anyone else. You also are a unique and different person. You are different to every other person on this planet! This means that you don't have to measure up to anyone else's standard for you. You don't have to conform. You are free to be you! The world waits to see the "you" that God created you to be.

My three daughters have my genes and my training, but somehow I didn't make them clones. They are all different. I would put each of them in the top ten of mothers, and yet each one of them mother their children differently. They discipline differently. They run their homes differently. They express themselves and order their lives according to the individual anointing that God placed in their hearts.

Dear mother, you don't have to try to be like someone else to find your identity. You don't even have to mother the same as a particular mother you admire, or according to some rules in a book. All you have to do is to mother according to your own heart and your individual personality. This is how you will be the best mother and the best homemaker. As a young mother, I remember reading that there is more in a mother's intuition than all the books you can ever read (although I am glad you are reading this one)!

Watching our first child grow, I couldn't wait for him to be like me. I expected him to love books and love to study! But no! He wasn't interested in reading books. He had a different personality. He had different interests. It took time for me to come to the realization that this was a person who was different from anyone else who had ever lived before and anyone else who would ever live again. My responsibility was not to make him measure up to my particular plans, but to look for the divine giftings God had given him and encourage him to grow into the person God planned him to be.

I often think of Lamech in Genesis 4:20-22 who had three sons and yet each one was uniquely different. Jabal was a cattleman and loved the animals and the outdoor life. Jubal was a musician and invented the harp and flute. Tubal-Cain opened the first foundry; he loved to work with his hands, forging instruments of bronze and iron. If I could have looked into the future when my children were little, I could never have imagined the things they are doing today. They are far more exciting, creative, and far-reaching than I could have planned.

Think about it. You were born to reflect a special image of God in this earth. You were born to reveal the creative love of God from your heart in a way that no one else can. Pour yourself out to touch others with God's love. Don't hold back. Don't deprive the world of seeing the unique hand of God upon your life.

Do the same for your husband. He doesn't have to be like you! Why not stop conforming him to your plans and let him be who God created him to be? It may be different to what you have planned, but it will better than your idea.

Do it for your children, too. This is the great challenge of parenting. You can't parent them all the same. God created each one individually!

Would you like to enter into this liberating path for you and your family? It will be challenging, but it will also take the pressure off your parenting! You will start to enjoy yourself.

One word of caution—you won't find who you are by looking into yourself. You will find your true identity as you pursue God and pour your life out for others. The more you know God the more you'll understand who He created you to be.

Prayer:

"My Creator, I thank you for making me special. You created me to worship you in a way that no one else will ever do. You created me to touch other people's lives in a way no one else can. You created me to bring glory to your wondrous name through the individuality you divinely imparted to me. I embrace how you made me and will no longer try to be like anyone else. Help me to also see my husband as the distinct person that he is. Help me to release my children to be the special individuals you created them to be. Amen."

Affirmation:

I am liberated and anointed to be the person God created me to be.

Day 55

Pay Them Back

Part 1

"If ye be reproached for the name of Christ, happy are ye,
for the spirit of glory and of God rests upon you"
(1 Peter 4:14).

Sometimes when ministering to women, I ask the question, "Who has never been hurt by something someone has said to them?" No one has ever raised a hand. All of us have been victims, at some time or other, of someone else's abuse, gossip, or hurting words. In fact, it is usually those who are closest to us, even family members, who hurt us the most. Words can be like arrows that pierce the soul to wound and destroy us.

I would like to tell you a secret. You don't have to stay wounded. There is a way out. God has provided kingdom principles for us, which if we obey them, will work miracles for us. They will free us from hurt and bitterness and enable us to live in total victory.

What are these kingdom principles?

1. Become Deaf and Dumb

I beg your pardon! Yes, that's what the Bible says.

Psalm 38:12-15 MLB says, *"They who seek my hurt talk mischief; they think up treacheries all day. But I am like a deaf man, who does not listen; like a dumb man, who does not open his mouth. Yes, I am like a man who does not hear and in whose mouth there are no arguments. For in Thee, Lord, I hope."*

DEAF. How curious we are to find out what people say against us. We want to track down every little morsel. However, God's way is to become deaf to what our accusers are saying. Can you master this challenge? What you don't know will save you from many hurts. Someone could be saying very nasty things about you, but if you don't know about it, you can relate to them with love and freedom, which will pour coals of fire on their wickedness.

DUMB. When we hear accusations against us, we should act dumb, with no reproofs or arguments. This was Jesus' example in the face of accusation and trial . . .

"But Jesus held his peace" (Matthew 26:59-63).

"Jesus answered nothing . . . He answered never a word" (Matthew 27:11-14).

"He opened not his mouth" (Isaiah 53:7).

116

"When He was insulted, He did not answer back with an insult; when He suffered, He did not threaten, but placed His hopes in God" (1 Peter 2:21-23).

2. Rejoice and Leap for Joy

Matthew 5:11-12 says, *"**Blessed** are you, when men shall hate you, and when they shall separate you from their company, and shall reproach you, and cast out your name as evil, for the Son of man's sake. **Rejoice ye in that day, and leap for joy:** for behold your reward is great in heaven . . ."*

The literal meaning for "leap for joy" is to "jump, bound, and spring." Have you ever tried jumping and leaping when someone has said unkind and untrue things about you? Try it. It actually works. It bounces all the hurt out of you! Do I hear the floorboards shaking?

3. Love

Matthew 5:44 says, *"But I say unto you, love your enemies."*

One writer says, "If a little bit of love isn't effective, increase the dose." The remedy for the ineffectiveness of a little love is MORE LOVE. A Chinese proverb says, "Don't try to put out the fire of a load of hay with a cup of water!" The more you have been hurt, the more love and forgiveness you'll need to pour on! Sometimes you'll have to pour on buckets!

How can you do this when you don't feeling like loving your enemy one little bit? You have to move out of your flesh into Christ's love. Because He lives in you, His love resides in you. You can love with His love even when you don't feel like loving. Romans 5:5 says, *"The love of God is shed abroad in our hearts by the Holy Ghost which is given unto us."*

Prayer:

"Oh Lord, please help me to keep my mouth shut in the face of accusations. Take away all my arguments for I put my hope and trust in you. Thank you that you are my Defender. Amen."

Affirmation:

I am deaf to hurtful words and dumb to my accusers.

Day 56

Pay Them Back

Part 2

"Do not pay back evil with evil or cursing with cursing: instead, **pay back with a blessing**, *because a blessing is what God promised to give you when He called you"*
(1 Peter 3:8-9 GNB).

 Today we continue to find out God's kingdom principles for coping with hurts and unkind words.

4. Bless

You certainly don't feel like blessing someone when they have hurt you, do you? It's the opposite of how you feel. Your fleshly nature wants to pay them back by hurting them like they have hurt you. God wants us to pay them back, but He wants us to *"pay them back with a blessing"* as many translations say.*

God wants us to retaliate too, but to *"retaliate with a blessing"* as the New English Bible translates it. We must get into the habit of hitting back with a "blessing reaction." Blessing is a kingdom principle that has power to set you free. I have proved it many times over the years. It always works.

Here are some more Scriptures:

"Bless them that curse you" (Matthew 5:44).

"Bless them which persecute you, bless, and curse not" (Romans 12:14).

"Bless—that's your job, to bless. You'll be a blessing and also get a blessing" (1 Peter 3:8-9, The Message).

"Being slandered, we bless" (1 Corinthians 4:12).

When someone speaks against you or hurts you, get down on your knees and bless them. You won't feel like it, but forget your feelings. Do it by faith. Keep blessing them. Don't get up off your knees until you know that when you meet them you can look them in the eye and bless them personally. In 1 Peter 3:8 the word "blessing" is not a noun, but a participle and should read, "be constantly blessing." Often you have to bless a person who has spoken against you many times before you are truly free in your spirit. You think you have the victory when suddenly all the hurt comes back again. What do you do? Keep on blessing. Don't give up blessing them until you are totally free of all hurt.

This is the power of blessing—you free the person who has hurt you, but you also free your own heart of bitterness and hurt. You get blessed by blessing because God's principles always work!

The Greek word for "bless" is *eulogeo* which means "to speak well of, to invoke a benediction upon, to cause to prosper."

5. Do Good

Matthew 5:44 reminds us to *"Do good to them that hate you."*

Can you think of something good you could do for the one who has hurt you? This is the opposite of what you feel like doing, but if you put God's principle into operation, you will see miracles happen.

6. Pray

Matthew 5:44 continues with more wisdom, *"Pray for them which despitefully use you, and persecute you."*

How much time in prayer do you spend for those who speak against you?

Prayer:

"Oh God, you are the Blesser of all mankind. You bless me even when I don't deserve it. Please help me to bless those who are unkind and speak hurtfully to me. Help me to walk in the power of this kingdom principle. Amen."

Affirmation:

Blessing is my way of life,
It's the way I put down strife!

*(Good News Bible, Jerusalem Bible, New Living Translation, J.B. Phillip's translation).

Day 57

Pay Them Back

Part 3

"Peter came to Jesus and asked, 'Lord, if my brother keeps on sinning against me, how many times do I have to forgive him? Seven times?' 'No, not seven times,' answered Jesus, 'but seventy times seven'"
(Matthew 18:21-22 GNB).

Today we check out the last four kingdom principles for coping with unkind words and deeds that people do to us.

7. Forgive

Matthew 6:14-15 says, *"If you will forgive others their trespasses, your heavenly Father will forgive you too; but if you do not forgive people, neither will your heavenly Father forgive your trespasses."*

It is very easy to be unforgiving because it is part of our fleshly life. Sometimes we can forgive once. But, do we really have to forgive someone 490 times? Forgiveness needs to become a lifestyle. We can't afford the luxury of not forgiving because it destroys. It not only destroys the one you won't forgive, but even more hurtfully, it destroys you! It destroys your soul. In the end you become the one who is hurt the most.

God's way is to forgive—and God's way works. It releases us into freedom and joy. Read Matthew 18:21-35, Luke 17:3-4 and Ephesians 4:32.

8. Forget

Hebrews 10:17 says, *"Their sins and iniquities will I remember no more."*

When God forgives our sins, He remembers them no more. What an example for us. When we forgive, we must also forget. That's the hard part. To help you forget, don't talk about your grievance. Every time you talk about it, you stir up the wound. You will soon forget if you don't talk about it all the time.

And remember to forgive and forget before you go to sleep at night (Ephesians 4:26).

9. Provide for their Needs

Romans 12:20-21 says, *"Therefore if thine enemy hunger, feed him; if he thirst, give him drink: for in so doing thou shalt heap coals of fire on his head. Be not overcome of evil, but overcome evil with good."*

Read also Proverbs 24:17-18 and 25:21-22 and ask God what He wants you to do.

10. Let God Vindicate

Romans 12:19 says, *"Vengeance is mine; I will repay, says the Lord."*

We dare not take from God what is His rightful authority. Only God has the authority to avenge. It is His right and He is the only one who can do it with pure judgment. You can trust God to do righteously and act on your behalf.

When you bless those who hurt you, you overcome three enemies at once:

THE DEVIL, who will take advantage of a hurt and unforgiving spirit and get a foothold in your life. Proverbs 18:14 says, *"A wounded spirit, who can bear?"* It will destroy your life. But, as you pray and bless the one who has wounded you, your spirit will become free.

YOUR ENEMY, the one who has hurt you. Many times it is someone very close to you—that's when it hurts the most! But, as you bless them, God will work in their hearts to change their attitude.

YOURSELF. This is the greatest victory of all. As you forgive and bless, you will be cleansed, healed, and blessed yourself. Your words and attitudes are boomerangs that always come back to you.

> It is not in your nature to bless those who have hurt you,
> but it is Christ's nature and He lives in you.

Prayer:

"Father God, I don't have it in myself to live by your kingdom principles, but I thank you that you live in me. Help me to live my life by the power of your life—loving, forgiving, and blessing. Amen."

Affirmation:

Because God forgives, I can forgive; because God forgets, I can forget.

Day 58

Leave Your Problems at the Door

"You shall call your walls Salvation, and your gates Praise"
(Isaiah 60:18).

I love the fact that our God is such a practical God. He is concerned about our everyday lives. He is even interested in the doors and the gates of our home. In fact, they are very important to Him and He speaks a lot about them. Psalm 87:2 tells us, *"The Lord loves the gates of Zion."* He loves your gates and doors, too.

Beautiful gates and doors fascinate me. When visiting my niece in Majorca a few years ago, I snapped most of my pictures of gates and doors—amazing huge wooden doors of all beautiful designs. It was also delightful to walk through the narrow streets of old villages. Old quaint doors and interesting gates led into courtyards, gardens, and homes. Doors are enticing. They are entrances that lead you into new adventures, new ideas, new vision, and new excitement—and of course into your home.

Praise Your Way In

God wants us to call the gates and doors of our home *Praise*. A good idea is to praise the Lord every time you enter a door of your home. Pray a short prayer of praise each time you open a door. "Thank you for this room. I enter into it with thanksgiving. Fill this room with your presence and love. Amen." Of course, many times you may be in a hurry. At least say, "Hallelujah: or "Praise the Lord" as you enter. Can you imagine the change in the atmosphere of your home if you praised your way into every room you enter? 2 Chronicles 31:2 tells us how Hezekiah the King appointed the Levites *"to give thanks and to praise in the gates."*

It may take time to get into the habit of doing this. I'm trying myself. Share the idea with your husband and children, too. You can remind one another until it becomes the habit of your lives.

Leave Your Burdens Behind

God gives us another practical principle about our doors in Jeremiah 17:19-27. Take time to read the whole passage. He told Jeremiah to go to all the gates of Jerusalem and tell the people that they were to take no burden through the gates of Jerusalem on the Sabbath day. They were not to carry a burden out of their houses either. Jeremiah spoke of the literal Sabbath day. However, through Jesus' death on the cross, God has now provided a way for us to live in a continual Sabbath rest. Jesus is our rest. He wants us to live in His rest. He wants us to have rest in our homes. He does not want our homes to be filled with tension, stress, bickering, and fighting.

He gives the remedy. Every time you enter a gate or door of your home, make sure you leave your burdens behind. Don't take them in with you. These burdens spoil the atmosphere of your home. They devour your home. Roll them over to Jesus at the door. He has promised to take your burdens and carry your sorrows (Psalm 55:22).

This passage in Jeremiah promises that if you do not take your burdens through the doors of your home that the King will sit on the throne! Who do you want ruling your home? Your problems and burdens? Or, King Jesus, who is your Rest forever? It's your choice.

Prayer:

"Oh Lord, please remind me to praise my way through every door of my home. I thank you that you are my Burden Bearer and that I don't have to carry my problems into my home with me. Help me to get in the habit of rolling them upon you before I enter the door of my home. Amen."

Affirmation:

Doors are my praise opportunity!

God Comes Down

*"**I am come down** to deliver them out of the hand of the Egyptians,
and to bring them up out of that land unto a good land and a large,
unto a land flowing with milk and honey"*
(Exodus 3:8).

God is high and lifted up above all, yet He comes down to where we are.
Psalm 113:6 tells us that He *"humbles himself to behold the things that are in the
heavens and in the earth."* David the Psalmist is in awe as he asks the question,
"What is man that you are mindful of him, and the son of man that you visit him"
(Psalm 8:4)? God wants to become personally involved in our lives.

When God came to deliver the children of Israel, He *"came down"* to them.
He came right down to where they were suffering and made bare His mighty
right arm on their behalf. God will also *"come down"* to you, into the midst of
your life, your home, and your circumstances.

Are you feeling despair, frustration, and helplessness? Cry out to the Lord.
He will come down to you. He will manifest Himself to you. He will come
right down to you in the midst of your "overwhelmingness." He wants to come
right into your kitchen.

There is no situation too low to which God will not come down! How far
does He come down?

He comes down to the dunghill for the needy and beggar
(1 Samuel 2:8 and Psalm 113).

He comes down to the dust for the poor
(1 Samuel 2:8 and Psalm 113:7).

He comes down into the horrible pit to those who are stuck in the slimy
mud of despair
(Psalm 40:1-2).

He comes down to the broken-hearted
(Psalm 34:18; 51:17; 147:3, Isaiah 61:1 and Luke 4:18).

He comes down to those who are held captive by Satan
(Leviticus 26:13; Psalm 68:6; 107:13-14; 146:7; Isaiah 42:7 and 61:1).

He comes down to those who are mourning
(Isaiah 57:18; 61:2-3 and Matthew 5).

He comes down to the lonely and forsaken.
(Psalm 68:6 and Isaiah 54:6).

He comes down to those are bowed down and overwhelmed
(Psalm 145:14).

He comes down to those who are hungry and need food
(Ruth 1:6 and Psalm 146:7).

He comes down to those who are infertile
(Genesis 21:1; 29:32 and 1 Samuel 2:21).

Why does God come down? God said in Exodus 3:16-17, "*I have **surely visited you**, and seen that which is done to you in Egypt: and I have said, **I will bring you up out of** the affliction of Egypt unto . . . a land flowing with milk and honey.*" He came down to the children of Israel to deliver them out of their bondage and bring them into a large place. God comes down to your need, not to grovel with you, but to lift you up! To bring you out! To set you free!

Prayer:

"*Dear Father God, I thank you that you come down to meet me in my need. I thank you that you are such a wonderful and personal God. Please help me to keep a soft and humble heart before you, because even though you dwell in the high and holy place, you promise to come down to revive the heart of the contrite ones. Thank you, Lord. Amen.*"

Affirmation:

"*God comes down to our lowest to lift us to his highest. He comes down to our saddest to lift us to His joyfullest. He comes down to our helplessness to succor with His great might.*"
~ *F. B. Meyer*

Day 60

What Do You Fear?

"You have become Sarah's children if you do what is right
without being frightened by any fear"
(1 Peter 3:6 Weymouth).

We know that healthy fear for preservation is God-given. But, there are also deceptive fears, and Satan uses these fears as one of his big tactics. You've got to watch out for them.

One of the greatest strategies of the enemy is to bind us up with fear even when there is no valid reason for the fear at all. Have you ever read Psalm 53:5? It says, *"There were they in great fear, where no fear was."* The margin in my Bible says, *"They feared a fear!"* Isn't that ridiculous? Satan deceives us to fear a fear! That's right. It's not reality. It's just the fear of a fear. What deception!

When you understand Satan's schemes, you can guard yourself from being hoodwinked. Let's read some more Scriptures:

Job 15:21 says, *"The sound of fears is in his ears."* It was not a real fear, just the sound of a fear. We constantly hear the sound of fears. We hear a negative verdict from the medical profession. If you are an older mother, you are told that you may have a Down syndrome baby . . . and so on. These negatives are not always facts. They are speculations as to what "might happen." We have to decide. Are we going to base our life on what "might happen" and be tortured by the "sound of fears," or are we going to trust in God, who is sure, steadfast, and able to deliver us in any situation?

Job 3:25 says, *"For the thing which I greatly feared is come upon me, and that which I was afraid of is come unto me."* Let's look at the Hebrew words more closely. "The thing *(pachad)* which I greatly feared *(pachad)* is come upon me." In other words, he "feared a fear!" He didn't fear a reality, but a fear, and the fear had power to overcome his life.

E. Stanley Jones says, "Nothing that can happen to you will be as bad as the fear itself." Francis of Sales said, "Fear is a greater pain than pain itself."

Whooping cough was an epidemic when one of my daughters was a little baby. I feared that she would get it, and she did! What I feared came upon me. Another time an epidemic was going through our city. I was at home with my children and somehow I didn't hear about it until after it was all over. None of my children came down with the sickness. I believe it was because I didn't hear about it and therefore didn't fear it. It's amazing the power spoken words can have upon us if we let the fear take hold.

1 Peter 3:6 tells us that we will be Sarah's daughters if we are not afraid. The word "afraid" in the Greek is *phobeo* which means "to run away, to be frightened, to be full of trepidation." Is this where we get the word, *phobia*?

Isaiah 51:13 NASB states, *"You fear continually all day long because of the fury of the oppressor . . . but where is the fury of the oppressor?"* Where is the fear you fear? Is it truly a reality or only in your imagination? Don't allow yourself to be trapped by deceptive fears. If you fear a fear that is not valid, stamp it out in the power of the name of Jesus. 2 Timothy 1:7 says, *"God has not given us a spirit of fear; but of power, and of love, and of a sound mind."*

Prayer:

"Oh Father, please help me to be aware of the deceptions of the enemy. Please show me when I fear a fear that is not reality. Help me to remember that fear does not come from you. Amen."

Affirmation:

E. Stanley Jones says, "Fear is self-centered, faith is God centered." I will be God centered rather than turning inward to invalid fears.

Day 61

God is Close to the Broken-Hearted

"The Lord is nigh unto them that are of a broken heart;
and saves such as be of a contrite spirit"
(Psalm 34:18).

Dear sweet mother, why do you cry?
Don't you know that your God is nigh?
He is closer to you than your very breath,
He will never forsake you, not even in death.

He created you for His joy and pleasure
And has chosen you as a special treasure.
He has graven your name on His very own palm,
He'll come to your aid with His mighty right arm.

He is your Source, He will fill your cup,
When you are down, He will lift you up.
You don't have to stay sad, for He is your Joy,
He'll help you conquer those things that annoy.

God has given you children, which are your glory
To enrich your life and help write your story.
You're in God's perfect will, this is your calling,
He'll help you each day and keep you from falling.

You can't do it alone, your strength is weak,
Trust in the Lord and things won't seem so bleak.
Look to the Lord, not the problems you face,
You'll be amazed the way He gives you His grace.

A joyful mother is what He wants you to be,
Filling your home with gladness and glee,
Counting your blessings and praising the Lord
For His daily mercies and love out-poured.

Psalm 30:5 says, *"Weeping may endure for a night, but joy comes in the morning."*

Prayer:

"Oh God, I thank you that you know when my heart is broken and that you feel my pain. I thank you that you have promised to come close to me in these times. I thank you for your nearness and comfort. Amen."

Affirmation:

"There is a place of comfort sweet, near to the heart of God;
A place where we our savior meet, near to the heart of God."
~ Cleland Boyd McAfee

Day 62

Power for Patience!

"Strengthened with all might, according to his glorious power, unto all patience and longsuffering with joyfulness; giving thanks unto the Father"
(Colossians 1:11-12).

Do you need more of God's power in your life? Do you need more of His power to help you mother each day? I have wonderful news for you. As you allow Him, God's power is working in you mightily. Not ordinary power, but the *dunamis* power of God, the power of God which releases miracles. It is the *dunamis* power of God which was poured out upon the disciples when they received the Holy Spirit to take the Gospel to the uttermost part of the earth (Acts 1:8). This is where we get the word *dynamite*—explosive power!

How easily we become deadened to the knowledge of the truth, the truth of God's power that works in us. Let's read some other Scriptures:

Ephesians 1:18-19, *"The eyes of your understanding being enlightened; that ye may know . . . what is the exceeding greatness of his power (dunamis) to us-ward who believe, according to the working of his mighty power, which he wrought in Christ when he raised him from the dead . . ."*

Ephesians 3:16, *"That he would grant you, according to the riches of his glory, to be strengthened with might (dunamis) by his Spirit."*

Ephesians 3:20, *"Now unto him that is able to do exceeding abundantly above all that we ask or think, according to the power (dunamis) that works in us."*

2 Timothy 1:7, *"For God hath not given us the spirit of fear; but of power (dunamis), and of love, and of a sound mind."*

2 Peter 1:3, *"According as his divine power (dunamis) hath given unto us all things that pertain unto life and godliness."*

But we haven't finished yet! It is not only *dunamis* power, but God's "glorious" power. This is the Greek word *doxa* which means "the perfection of God's divine nature, the revelation of who He is."

People pray for power to witness for Christ, to heal the sick, and to do mighty miracles in the name of the Lord. But let's read Colossians 1:11 again. What is the purpose of God's *dunamis* power working in our lives? **To be patient and longsuffering!** That's the message!

Do you have trouble being patient? Are you plagued with anger? You do not have to be defeated any longer. Jesus died on the cross to give you the victory. Jesus Christ, the Son of God, did not die in vain. He died to not only save you from your sin, but to deliver you from your "self" nature and to change you into the image of His Son. His *dunamis* power is working in you mightily to reveal God's nature and character in you and through you—to your husband, your children, and to the people you associate with in your life.

Let Him work in you mightily. Jesus' blood has been shed to give you a new life. You can have patience because Christ lives in you and He is patient! You can have longsuffering because Christ in you is longsuffering. He does not fly off the handle! He does not scream and shout! He has long patience and forbearance. And His wonderful life is living in you! Acknowledge it. Confess it. Read Galatians 2:20 and Colossians 1:27.

We still haven't finished! Not only is Christ living His patient and long-suffering nature in you, but He enables you to do it with **joy and thankfulness**. Christ in you is **joy**. In the flesh you live in defeat, but in Christ you can bear your burdens with joy. You can put up with those who would naturally drive you mad. You can be patient with your children. You can endure as the power of God works in you mightily.

Prayer:

"Father, open my eyes to see
Jesus living His life in me! Amen."

Affirmation:

The patience of Jesus is in me; therefore I am patient!

Hasty Words

"I said in my haste, I am cut off from before thine eyes: nevertheless thou heardest the voice of my supplications when I cried unto thee"
(Psalm 31:22).

How easy it is to say things in haste! We spout off before we think. Usually when we speak hastily it is out of reaction. We often don't even believe the words we say! But, sad to say, we say them, and words have power! They have power to hurt our husband and our children. Charles Spurgeon says, "Hasty words are but for a moment on the tongue, but they often lie for years on the conscience."

I remember with shame an incident that happened in the early days of our marriage. I felt hurt by words my husband spoke to me and hastily retorted, "You should have married someone else!" Fortunately, I have a husband who doesn't let things go uncovered. He came to me a little later and said, "Do you believe in the power of words?" "Yes," I muttered. "Well, you better take back what you said," he stated firmly. I realized he was right and I had to retract and confess my hasty words.

Hasty words are often words of doubt because we have not given time for faith to grow or for God to move. We often have to wait for God. David cries out that he is cut off from the Lord, but he soon finds that they were hasty words as God had heard his cry all along. We must give God time to answer. His timing and His way is always the best way.

I cringe when I hear folk speaking derogatively against the Lord because things are not going the way they want. Again Spurgeon says, "Unbelief will have a corner of the heart of the firmest believer, and out of that corner it will vent many spiteful things against the Lord if the course of providence be not quite so smooth as nature might desire. Forever be such dark suspicions banished from our minds."

Proverbs 29:20 is also a challenging Scripture, *"Seest thou a man who is hasty in his words? There is more hope of a fool than him."*

Ecclesiastes 5:2 says, *"Be not rash with thy mouth, and let not thine heart be hasty to utter anything before God: for God is in heaven, and thou upon earth: therefore let thy words be few."* How true it is that the more words we speak the more opportunity we have to sin. Read Proverbs 10:19 and 17:28.

How do we stop these hasty words? James 1:19 says, *"Let every man be swift to hear, slow to speak, slow to wrath."* We want to be *"slow to speak"* but how do we do it? I believe we have to get into the **habit** of doing it. Each time someone "rubs you up the wrong way," shut your mouth. Wait before you speak. If you can't think of anything positive to say, don't say anything at all. That's what Jesus did. When they accused Him, He answered nothing. He didn't even open His mouth (Matthew 27:13-14). Is that the hardest thing you've ever tried to do? You can do it if you *will* to do it, especially as you ask the Lord to help you.

You will often fail. But keep working on making it a habit of your life. Some people say it takes 30 days to break a habit. Some say it takes 21 days to establish a habit. However, some habits may take a lot longer. Never despair. Keep trying and keep looking to the Lord who is your source. He lives in you and He is full of self control (Galatians 5:22-23). Continually ask the Holy Spirit to work in your heart *and your tongue*. He will work His grace in you.

Proverbs 4:23, *"Keep thy heart with all diligence: for out of it are the issues of life."*

Prayer:
"Lord, please help me not to be hasty in my words. Help me to trust you in each situation rather than reacting out of my emotions. Amen."

Affirmation:
My words determine the course of my life and my family.

Day 64

Hold on to Your Crown

*"Behold, I come quickly: hold that fast which thou hast,
that no man take thy crown"*
(Revelation 3:11).

When God appeared to Moses as I AM THAT I AM out in the backside of the desert, He commissioned him to deliver the Hebrews from their slavery in Egypt. But Moses was fearful to take on such a task. He had no strength of his own to accomplish it. God then said to him, *"What is that in thine hand, Moses?"* (Exodus 4:2).

What was in his hand? A shepherd's rod. Nothing fancy. Nothing powerful. Just a simple rod he used each day to guide, prod, and protect his flock. God took that ordinary shepherd's rod and made it a mighty weapon in Moses' hand. Whenever he stretched forth the rod, mighty miracles happened. It released the plagues upon the Egyptians. It showed forth God's mighty power.

Sometimes you wonder what you are doing in your home. Your friends have high-powered careers and are raking in the money. You are trying to make ends meet from day to day. People around you tell you that you are wasting your life and your education.

But, what is in your hand? It is the rod of motherhood. It may look insignificant, as Moses' rod did, but it wields a mighty power. Motherhood is the most powerful career in the nation. As a mother, you determine the course of the nation. You are in God's hands preparing your children for the purposes God has laid out for them before the foundation of the world. This is a top notch job. It is a high-powered career!

Mothering is your crown. It has been invested in you by God himself. It is your anointing of womanhood. It is your authority. Do not take off your beautiful crown of motherhood to allow someone else to mother the children God has given you.

You may be going through circumstances that make you feel like giving up. You feel like an utter failure. You feel like this mothering business is not working out. Your children are giving you heartache. Do not give up, dear mother. Hold on to your crown and never let it go. Lift your head high and be proud of your divine calling. Rise up in the motherhood anointing and authority that God has given you.

Do not let other people rob you either. Revelation 3:11 tells us that man will try to take your crown from you. Those who are ignorant of God's heart for children will speak negative things into your life. Those who are deceived by this world's philosophy will try to lure you away from your high calling. Do not be swayed by what people say. Hold on to your crown tightly. Do not for a moment be intimidated by your antagonists (Philippians 1:28)!

Prayer:

"Father, I thank you that you have given me the crown of mothering. Help me to remember each day that it is a crown of which I can be proud. When I wear this crown I am walking in your perfect will. Amen."

Affirmation:

Mothering is a crown I wear with dignity.

What is in Thine Hand?

"What is that, oh Christian mother
God hath 'trusted to thy care?
In thine hand to love and nurture,
Sweetly innocent and fair!

What a high and noble privilege!
Bring them up to know God's Word;
They in turn will call thee blessed
When they've learned to trust the Lord!"
~ Mary A. Haydon

Day 65

God Knows Your Sorrows

*"And the Lord said, **I have surely seen the affliction** of my people which
are in Egypt, and have **heard their cry** by reason of their taskmasters; for **I
know their sorrows**; and I am come down to deliver them out of the hand of
the Egyptians . . . behold, the cry of the children of Israel is come unto me: and
I have also **seen the oppression** wherewith the Egyptians oppress them"*
(Exodus 3:7, 9).

I know your sorrows!" There could not be any more comforting words that you
could hear from your loving Heavenly Father.

Are you going through a time of sorrow in your life? God says to you,
"I know your sorrows." He **feels** your heartache. He has not forgotten you.
Hebrews 4:15 reminds us that we have a High Priest who is *"touched with the
feeling of our infirmities."* He sympathizes with your weaknesses.

Have you been crying out with anguish and grief? God says to you, "I **hear**
your cry. I see your tears." His ears are open to you. Psalm 56:8 TLB says, *"You
have seen me tossing and turning through the night. You have collected all my tears
and preserved them in your bottle! You have recorded every one in your book."* Read
also Psalm 116:8; 126:5-6 and Isaiah 25:8.

Are you in a situation where you feel you are under servitude? Do you feel
you are in a prison from which you can't escape? Are you groaning under hard
bondage as did the children of Israel? God says to you, "I **see** your oppression."
The eyes of the Lord run to and fro over the whole earth. He sees what is
going on in your life and in your home.

"But," you answer, "if God sees my heartache and hears my cry to Him,
why doesn't He do something about it? I'm still suffering."

God had not forgotten His people in Egypt. He knew their sorrows. He
watched over their afflictions year after year. Although they lived in Egypt
for 430 years, historians believe that their persecution began about a hundred
years before their deliverance. They could have lived under persecution for a
whole century, although it intensified in the latter years. But, God was not
deaf to their cries of anguish as they endured their bitter slavery. He had His
perfect timing. In fact, He was already working! He was preparing a leader and
it couldn't be done in a moment. He spent 40 years preparing Moses out in
the desert, and at the right moment, He brought His deliverer upon the scene.

Dear mother, do not despair as you wait for God to answer your cry. God is already working, although you may not see it yet. He will bring His deliverance in His perfect timing. Wait for God's moment for then it will be a true deliverance. God does not always do His work in haste. He does a thorough work and it often takes time. It takes time for Him to complete His work in us. It takes time for Him to perform His work of grace in those who affect our lives.

I pray that you will be comforted and encouraged by these beautiful promises:

Psalm 22:24 NLT, *"For He has not ignored the suffering of the needy. He has not turned and walked away. He has listened to their cries for help."*

Psalm 31:7 NLT, *"For you have seen my troubles, and you care about the anguish of my soul."*

Psalm 34:18 NLT, *"The Lord is close to the broken-hearted, he rescues those who are crushed in spirit."*

Psalm 40:1-2 MLB, *"I waited and waited for the Lord; then **He bent over to me*** (How tender! How personal! How wonderful!) *and heard my cry. He brought me up from a destructive pit, from the miry clay, and set my feet on a rock, steadying my steps."*

Trust Him, dear one. He knows and understands your sorrows.

Prayer:

"Thank you, dear God and Father, that you know and understand the grief and heartache I am going through. I thank you that you are my faithful High Priest and you feel my oppression. I thank you that you are working on my behalf right now. I trust you, Lord. I submit my life to you, knowing that you understand my sorrow and will work out your perfect will in my life. Amen."

Affirmation:

I trust God's timing. It may be later than my timing, but it will be the perfect timing.

Further Reading:

Read also Genesis 50:24-25; Exodus 4:31; Deuteronomy 26:6-9; Nehemiah 9:9; Psalm 106:43-45; Isaiah 63:9 and Acts 7:34.

It's Not as Bad as You Think

"In everything give thanks for this is the will of God in Christ Jesus concerning you"
(1 Thessalonians 5:18).

It's easy to feel sorry for yourself, isn't it? I think it's the easiest thing to do in the world. Yet, it is the most debilitating—and the most deceiving. Our mind takes us down a road that makes everything seem far worse than it really is.

I remember one time when my children were all small. I was at the kitchen sink doing the dishes and I began a self-pity trip. I was feeling so sorry for myself that the tears rolled down my face. I was really in the pit! Then I looked up. There was my Bible open at Psalm 103. Fortunately, I had established the habit of having my Bible open at my windowsill. In those days, with all my little children around me, I didn't have much time to sit and read the Bible. Instead, I would grab a verse from Psalms or Proverbs as I worked in my kitchen.

I read verses 2–5, *"Bless the Lord, O my soul, and forget not all his benefits: who forgives all your iniquities, who heals all your diseases, who redeems your life from destruction, who crowns you with lovingkindness and tender mercies, who satisfies your mouth with good things . . ."*

All at once, I realized what I was doing. I was totally deceived. I had let my mind get out of control. I had to gird up the loins of my mind. I repented. "Oh Lord, I am so sorry. Forgive me for my self-centeredness. Oh Lord, I thank you for all your blessings. Thank you for all your goodness to me. Thank you for my salvation. Thank you for my husband. Thank you for the children you have given me. Thank you for this home you have provided for me. Thank you that you are my God and you are watching over me."

As I thanked the Lord, the self-pity left me and once again I walked in victory.

My daughter, Pearl, shares a similar experience. She was sitting in her little trailer home feeling very sorry for herself. She thought, "I deserve a bigger home than this. I haven't been able to buy new clothes for months. I have nothing nice and pretty to wear." The more she thought about it, the more miserable she became.

In the middle of her misery, her little boy (about 10 months at the time) came up and gave her a big hug. He gave her the biggest smile with his little grubby face. Right then her heart burst open with joy. She realized that she had everything she needed. God had given her two beautiful children and she had a third one growing in her womb. She had a husband who loved her. What more did she need? She had more than she deserved. As she began to thank the Lord, all the material aspirations left her and she wrote the song, *My Heart is Full*. Instead of being full of self-pity, she was now full of thankfulness to God for His blessings.

Dear mother, when you start falling into that slough of self-pity, stop! Don't keep sliding down. Look up to the Lord. Start thanking Him for all His blessings. They are numberless. They are more than you can count. When you start praising instead of complaining, joy will fill your heart.

Prayer:

"Father God, please save me from being self-centered. I repent of my selfish ways and thoughts. Please convict me and arrest me when I get into self-pity. Lead me out of self and into you. Amen."

Affirmation:

I'm praising in the good times and the bad!

My Heart is Full:

To hear Serene and Pearl sing this song, go to:
http://aboverubies.org/PeaceAllOverMeMp3

Day 67

Have You Dedicated Your Home?

Part 1

"What man is there who has built a new house and has not dedicated it?
Let him go and return to his house, lest he die in the battle
and another man dedicate it"
(Deuteronomy 20:5).

When King Solomon spoke to King Huram of Tyre about materials for building a temple for the living God, he confessed, *"Behold, I build an house to the name of the Lord my God, to dedicate it to Him"* (2 Chronicles 2:4). He was speaking of building a temple for God to dwell. There is no temple left today, but God now wants to dwell in our bodies, which are temples of the Holy Spirit. He also wants to dwell in our homes.

Have you dedicated the house you live in to the Lord? It may be a new home, or a home you have purchased from someone else. Either way, you need to dedicate it to the Lord. It is especially important to cleanse and dedicate a home that has had previous owners. You cannot know what has taken place in the home and you don't want to give the slightest opportunity for Satan to take a foothold in your home.

The owner of every new house in Israel made a celebration and dedicated it to the Lord. Speaking of the Israelites dedicating their homes, Samuel Chandler writes, "It was common when any person had finished a house and entered into it, to celebrate it with great rejoicing, and keep a festival, to which his friends are invited, and to perform some religious ceremonies, to secure the protection of Heaven." John Calvin writes, "By consecrating their houses to God, they declared that they were God's tenants, confessing that they were strangers, and that it was He who lodged, and gave them a habitation."

If you haven't already set apart your home, don't wait any longer. Put on a feast, gather in some friends and ask them to pray with you over your home. Walk into every room and ask God to cleanse it and for His power to flow into the room. Invoke God's blessing over every inch of your home and set it apart for His presence and His purposes.

Or, when your friends move into a new or used home, give them a surprise celebration. Gather friends, take food for a feast, gifts for their new home, and bless their home with them. When I was young, growing up in New Zealand, people gave a Tin Canning to a new married couple when they moved into their home. They called it a Tin Canning because people took jars of food they had canned and loaded the young couple with food for the coming year.

In parts of the United States, they call the same celebration a Pounding. I guess this was because everyone took a pound of something to the new couple, e.g. a pound of sugar, flour, butter, cake, or whatever they had available. This is a wonderful way to bless a new married couple, but more importantly, to take the opportunity to dedicate and set apart the home.

If you are a songwriter, you could write a song for your new home, or you could write a song for someone else as they go into their new or used home. King David, the Psalmist of Israel, wrote a song of thanks and praise when he moved into his new home in Jerusalem. The title of Psalm 30 says, *"A Psalm and Song at the dedication of the house of David."*

When King Solomon and the children of Israel dedicated the house of the Lord, Solomon put on a great feast that lasted for 14 days (1 Kings 8:62-66)! Set apart your home with feasting, singing, and prayers of dedication.

Prayer:

"Lord, please help me to be aware each new day that my home belongs to You. Help me to see it as a holy temple for your presence. Amen."

Affirmation:

My home is a sanctuary for the living God.

Day 68

Have You Dedicated Your Home?

Part 2

"The Lord is my strength and song, and he is become my salvation:
*he is my God, and **I will prepare him a habitation**"*
(Exodus 15:2).

What a mighty vision! It would be hard to find anything more significant in life than to make your home a habitation for the living God. When you dedicate your home to God, you are setting it apart as a holy place. This involves more than an initial celebration; it takes daily work.

Hyman Goldin writes, "Every home can thus be turned into a holy shrine where godliness prevails . . . every member of the family is a priest unto God; the home is a shrine; and the table is an altar of God." We need to get into the habit of being consciously aware that our home is a sanctuary for God. When we have this vision before us, we will be more likely to work at keeping it a holy place. We will have the vision to make our home not only a haven of love, peace, and joy for our family, but a sanctuary for God's presence.

We will see our table as a consecrated place to establish the family altar each day, where we open the Word of God and pray together. Oh for godly homes all across this nation, sitting at the table to eat their meals together. Not only eating together, but also enjoying Family Devotions where they pray for one another and for the nation. Can you imagine what could happen in our nation if Christian families all across the country began to pray together at their Family Altar? Not only the fathers and mothers praying, but each one of the children, crying out to God for His mercy and salvation upon the nation!

Have you established the Family Altar in your home? This is the best way to daily dedicate your home to the Lord. We can't forget the old adage, "The family that prays together stays together."

What blessing for God's protecting, powerful eye to be upon our homes night and day. God has given us this promise. Actually, it was given for the temple that Solomon built for God's presence, but today God wants our homes to be temples filled with His presence. It is not a mandatory promise, but conditional. The promise is to those who will humble themselves, pray, seek God's face, and turn from their wicked ways. Yes, you know it, don't you? It's 2 Chronicles 7:14, but have you read on to verse 16? *"Now my eyes will be open and my ears attentive to prayer made in this place . . . my eyes and my heart will be there perpetually."*

If we are a humble, praying family, not only does God promise that He will forgive our sin and heal us, but He promises that He will keep His eye and His heart upon our home continually. There could be no greater blessing.

Do you want God's eyes and His heart to look perpetually on your home? Keep a humble spirit. Become a praying family. Pray together around your table at every breakfast and every evening meal.

Prayer:

"Peace, unto this house, I pray,
Keep terror and despair away;
Shield it from evil and let sin
Never find lodging room within.
May never in these walls be heard
The hateful or accusing word.
Amen."

Affirmation:

Our family prayers will impact the nation and the world.

Further Study:

*Go to www.aboverubies.org and under **Articles and Stories**, go to **The Family Meal Table**, **Prayer in the Home** and **Bible in the Home** where you will find over 50 articles and testimonies on the power of families reading God's Word and praying together.*

✦

Have You Dedicated Your Home?

Part 3

"When they had . . . consecrated themselves, they went in to purify the temple of the Lord, as the king had ordered, following the word of the Lord"
(2 Chronicles 29:15).

It is beneficial to frequently de-clutter your home of the junk that accumulates. It is even more important to regularly go through your home and check for anything that could defile your home. Check the magazines. Go through your bookshelf. Inspect your music. Check your children's rooms, too. What about ornaments, pictures, and gifts that you have accumulated? Are they glorifying to the Lord?

A good way to check whether to throw it out or keep it, is to line it up alongside Philippians 4:8.

1. Whatever is True

We must allow no deception in our homes. We must be transparent with one another—no hiding or deceiving.

2. Whatever is Honest

The Greek word is *semnos* which actually means "that which inspires respect and reverence." It has majestic and awe-inspiring qualities. Everything in our homes—pictures, décor, music, and atmosphere should promote majesty and reverence.

3. Whatever is Just and Right

Don't allow anything in your home that is on the borderline of righteousness. If it is questionable, throw it out!

4. Whatever is Pure

The word is *hagnos*, which means "freedom from defilements and impurities, especially sexual sin." Do not allow anything in your home that promotes lust or impurity. Guard your TV. Check every DVD that comes into your home. Guard your computers. It is too dangerous for children to have computers in their bedrooms, or husbands for that matter. They should be in the living room, in the open, where all can watch what appears on the screen.

5. Whatever is Lovely

Is your home light and sunshiny? Is the atmosphere lovely? Are your pictures lovely? I am sad when I see dubious and sensual pictures on the walls of Christian homes. Your children will be influenced by the pictures on your wall. I remember the story of a mother whose sons all chose to go to sea for their living. When someone asked them the reason, they pointed to the pictures on the walls, which were of ships on the ocean. Of course, there is nothing wrong with pictures of ships, but it reveals the influencing power of pictures.

I stayed in the home of a young mother and her walls were decorated with beautiful pictures of mothers and babies. Her eight children are surrounded with these lovely pictures that promote tenderness and maternity.

6. Whatever is of Good Report

Everything in our homes should be good—good words (don't allow negative, back-biting, morbid or discouraging words), good clean fun, good books, and good music.

7. Whatever is Excellent

This word, *arête*, is the same that is used in 1 Peter 2:9 where it says, "*We should show forth the praises* (excellencies and virtues) *of Him who has called you out of darkness into His marvelous light.*" Everything in our home should show forth the excellency of our holy God. It should reveal the beauties of His character. It is a holy place to the Lord.

8. Whatever is Worthy of Praise

Everything in our homes should uplift us and cause us to praise the Lord—décor, books, DVDs, and music.

God's Word is very strong about what we have in our homes. Deuteronomy 7:25-26 says, "*You shall burn the carved images of their gods with fire, you shall not covet the silver or gold that is on them, nor take it for yourselves, lest you are snared by it; for it is an abomination to the Lord your God. Nor shall you bring an abomination into your house, lest you be doomed to destruction like it; but you shall utterly detest and utterly abhor it, for it is an accursed thing.*" Read also Matthew 21:12-13 and Acts 19:19.

Set aside some time to de-clutter your home of all that does not line up with Philippians 4:8.

Prayer:

"Dear God, help me to remember daily that my home is a place for your glory to dwell. Help me to consistently cleanse my home of all the things that subtlety enter in to defile it. Amen."

Affirmation:

I am a temple cleanser!

THE DEAREST IDOL
The dearest idol I have known,
Whate'er that idol be,
Help me to tear it from thy throne,
And worship only thee.

So shall my walk be close with God,
Calm and serene my frame;
So purer light shall mark the road
That leads me to the Lamb.
~ William Cowper

Day 70

Don't Look Around—Look Up

"Be not dismayed; for I am your God"
(Isaiah 41:10).

The Hebrew word for "be dismayed" means "to gaze, to be non-plussed, to look around in amazement or bewilderment."

Where are you looking, dear mother? Are you looking in despair at all you have to do? Are you looking at the difficulties you face and worrying about how you can cope? Or, are you looking up? God, who is our Rock, our Fortress, our Savior, and our Deliverer specifically tells us to stop looking at what we see around us and instead to look to Him, even though we cannot see Him. He is God. He is in control. We can trust Him unreservedly with our lives and all our problems.

How can I do it? I have too much to do,
I'm overwhelmed and feeling real blue,
I'm stuck in this house like super glue.
Don't look around—LOOK UP!

The dishes and laundry are piled up high,
When I look 'round the house I have to sigh,
And for supper my husband's expecting a pie!
Don't look around—LOOK UP!

We can't pay the mortgage; bills are overdue,
I'm tired and have headaches, not a few,
These children are driving me crazy too!
Don't look around—LOOK UP!

My husband comes home late; he doesn't care,
He doesn't help with the children; it's not fair!
I don't want to smile; I just want to glare!
Don't look around—LOOK UP!

Take your eyes off your problems, look up to Him,
God's presence is with you, even in the din!
Confess your bad mood and He'll cleanse your sin.
He is your God—LOOK UP!

He will show you how to order your place,
He will give you direction as you seek His face,
He wants to pour upon you His anointing of grace.
He is your God—LOOK UP!

Keep your eyes fixed on Him; He is your Stay,
He is your Wisdom for problems each day,
He will bring His presence right into your fray.
He is your God—LOOK UP!

Each morning He comes as the refreshing Dew
To revive your body, and your spirit too,
He is your Deliverer and He'll make you new,
He is your God—LOOK UP!

Prayer:

"Oh God, forgive me for looking at everything, except you. Help me to remember that you are bigger than my circumstances and the problems that I face. I thank you that you are in control of my life and every situation. I look to you as my Source and my Deliverer. Amen."

Affirmation:

My eyes are upon God, not the troubling things around me.

Day 71

How's Your Self-Control?

"The fruit of the Spirit is . . . self control"
(Galatians 5:23).

Self control" is not a word we particularly like, is it? It gives the feeling of being in a straight jacket. But no, self-control is actually freedom. The one who has self-control is free to say "Yes" or free to say "No." The one who has self-control is free to walk in the Spirit rather than the flesh. The person who cannot resist temptation is the one who is in bondage.

Self-control does not mean we are regimented. Some people naturally live structured or even ascetic lives. Others are more relaxed and flow with whatever is happening. It is not talking about your personality type, but about Christ's life living through you.

The fruit of the Spirit is a picture of the life of Jesus. He mastered the temptations of the flesh. Jesus actually experienced the same temptations that we do, but overcame them. Hebrews 4:15 says, *"For we have not an high priest which cannot be touched with the feeling of our infirmities, but was in all points tempted like as we are, yet without sin."*

He mastered the desire to avoid the agony and suffering of the cross. Instead, He abandoned His life to God and embraced His Father's will. He became a lamb willingly led to the slaughter. It was not a small struggle. He sweat drops of blood as he fought the battle between the flesh and the spirit.

Because He suffered and faced temptation, He is able to help us in our temptations and struggles. Hebrews 2:18 says, *"For in that he himself hath suffered being tempted, he is able to succor them that are tempted."* Not only is He able to help us, but He lives in us by His Holy Spirit and His life is a life of self-control.

A friend of mine told me about her father who lived a very disciplined life. Three days a week he wore brown suits and ate eggs for breakfast. The other two days a week he wore blue suits and ate a sweet breakfast, never deviating from his schedule. And yet he was totally out of control morally.

Don't despair, dear mother. You may think you are unorganized as you minister to the needs of all your little ones. This is not the issue. The issue is whether **God is in control** of your life, not whether it is a structured or a "go with the flow" life.

Self-control is Christ control. It is allowing His life to live through you. It is acknowledging the power of His self-control, which is in you. This virtue has already been given to you. 2 Timothy 1:7 says, *"For God has not given us a spirit of cowardice, but of power and love and self-control."*

Self-control is not bondage. You are free to say "Yes." There is no law against it. This is what Galatians 5:22-25 tells us, *"The fruit of the Spirit* (the character of Christ) *is love, joy, peace, patience, kindness, goodness, faithfulness, gentleness, self-control; against such there is no law. And those who belong to Christ Jesus have crucified the flesh with its passions and desires. If we live by the Spirit, let us also walk by the Spirit."*

This is liberating truth. When your husband has hurt you and wounded you, you are free to love him back! There is no law against it! When someone is unkind to you, you are free to retaliate with gentleness and lovingkindness. There is not a law in the land against it! When the temptation of the flesh lures you, you are free to say "No" and walk in the Spirit instead. And nothing or nobody can stop you (except your own flesh)!

I remember reading years ago of a preacher who said, "Love God and do what you like." He was not talking about a weak, hypocritical Christian walk, but an intense passion and zeal for God. Love goes beyond all laws. If we love God with all our heart, mind, soul, and strength, we will only want to please Him. We will want to say "Yes" to Him. We won't need laws and regulations because we will want to walk in the Spirit and in holiness. Through the power of His self-control that is in us, we can walk away from the *"lust of the flesh, and the lust of the eyes, and the pride of life"* (1 John 2:15-17).

Prayer:

"Thank you, Lord, that you have come to indwell me by your Holy Spirit. Thank you, Lord that I do not have to work up self-control in my life. It is not my doing, but your doing. When you are in control of my life, I have self-control. I have the power to say "No" to the devil. I have the power to deny the cravings of the flesh. I am not in bondage but free to walk in the liberty of Christ who has set me free. Amen."

Affirmation:

Self-control is part of my life because Christ lives in me.

Home Destroyers

Part 1

"Having food and clothing, with these we shall be content"
(1 Timothy 6:8).

Reading through Proverbs recently I noticed that it mentions seven things that destroy the home. I prefer not to write about negative things, but, on the other hand, we can't sweep any of God's Word under the mat. And God's negatives always turn to positives. When we read His warning signs which mean ROAD BLOCK, WRONG WAY—GO BACK, or DEAD END we know that it is not the road to take, even though it looks like a beautiful and easy road. We must swerve back on to the road God has planned for us from the beginning of time. God has never changed his plans. His ways are still the only ones that work effectively. Jeremiah 6:16 says, *"Thus saith the Lord, Stand ye in the ways, and see, and ask for the old paths, where is the good way, and walk therein, and ye shall find rest for your souls."*

Let's look at some of these WRONG WAY signs.

1. Greediness

Proverbs 15:27 says, *"He that is greedy of gain troubles his own house."*

No wonder one of the Ten Commandments is, *"Thou shalt not covet thy neighbor's house . . . thou shalt not covet thy neighbor's wife . . . nor any thing that is thy neighbor's"* (Exodus 20: 17). When we see friends with things we don't have, it is easy to hanker after them, too. Most people like to be like everyone else and have everything that their associates have. We can become despondent and full of self-pity because we can't afford what we want. This takes away our joy of living and being *"content with such things as we have"* (Hebrews 13:5-6).

As we crave a better house and more things to put in the house, we start to plan how we can get these things. Ideas take shape. That's it! I could do what everyone else is doing who has more things. I could go out and get a job! Yes, that's the answer. But is it? To go out and get a job you have to leave the home behind. You have to vacate the very place where God wants you to be—in the heart of the home (Psalm 128:3). You have to put your children in daycare or leave them with someone else. God didn't give your children to you to give them to someone else to look after! He gives the responsibility to you. You are the only one who can truly nurture and nourish your baby and children.

The home becomes a show piece of material riches rather than filling it with the true riches of children. When you get your eyes on material riches, children become a nuisance, but children are eternal treasures. Material possessions are only for this life. Proverbs 23:4-5 says, *"Labor not to be rich: cease from thine own wisdom. Wilt thou set thine eyes upon that which is not? For riches certainly make themselves wings; they fly away as an eagle toward heaven."*

May God save us from a greedy spirit.

Prayer:

"Father, I pray that you will take every spirit of greediness from me. Give me a contented spirit. Help me to enjoy the riches you have given me—my precious children and the (little) house you have provided for me. I thank you for the blessing of food and clothing. Amen."

Affirmation:

Content in my home, that's for me,
With coveting gone, I'm now free!

Day 73

Home Destroyers

Part 2a

"For my people are foolish, they know me not; they are stupid children,
they have no understanding"
(Jeremiah 4:22 RSV).

The Bible tells us plainly that foolishness will pull down our home.

2. Foolishness

Proverbs 14:1 states, *"Every wise woman builds her house, but the foolish plucks it down with her hands."*

What does it mean to be foolish? Simply, it means to do it my way rather than God's way. God's way, although different to my way, always ends in blessing. My way, although it may look good, always ends in destruction.

If we are not building our home, we are pulling it down. How do we pull it down?

a) We pull down our home by vacating the home

God wants the mother in the home—nurturing, nourishing, and training her children. We can't do everything successfully. We either build up a business (usually someone else's business), or we build up our home. God has given us a full time job to tend our little flock. God gives a warning to the mother shepherdess when He says in Zechariah 11:17, *"Woe to the worthless shepherd, who leaves the flock!"* Notice that this Scripture has an exclamation mark!

b) We pull down our home by our words

Negative words. Critical words. Reactive words. Spiteful words. Angry words. And on it goes.

We either build up our home with words
or we destroy our home with words!

When God allowed Satan to get at His servant Job, He smote him with terrible boils from the top of his head to the sole of his feet. Job was in agony and pain. Instead of encouraging him, Job's wife said, *"Do you still hold on to your integrity? Curse God, and die."* Job replied, *"You speak as one of the foolish women*

153

speaks. Shall we indeed accept good from God, and shall we not accept adversity?" (Job 2:9-10).

Do you speak as one of the foolish women, or as one of the wise?

Sometimes it may not be negative words. It may be wasteful words. Proverbs 15:2 says, *"The mouth of fools pours forth foolishness."* Often we speak unnecessary words when we should keep our mouths shut. I am always challenged by Proverbs 10:19, *"In the multitude of words there wanteth not sin: but he that refraineth his lips is wise."* The more we blab on about anything and everything, the more opportunity there is to sin with our mouth. The NLT makes it clearer, *"Don't talk too much, for it fosters sin. Be sensible and turn off the flow!"*

c) We pull down our home by spending frivolously and unwisely
The foolish woman buys according to her whims and what takes her fancy. She buys groceries without thought for nutrition or without reading the ingredients. She fills her cupboards with devitalized packaged foods instead of cooking from scratch. She purchases unnecessary "things" to fill her home which could be used for wiser needs.

Proverbs 21:20 says, *"There is treasure to be desired and oil in the dwelling of the wise; but a foolish man (or woman) spendeth it up."* The foolish woman spends more than her husband can afford. The wise woman lives frugally within her means. I often had to remind my new adopted daughters that we don't have to eat what we want whenever we want. We must learn to live thriftily rather than extravagantly.

d) We pull down or home by wasting
Many women not only waste time but waste products. They throw out everything. It is not wise to be a hoarder and clutter up your home, but there are many things that can be re-used to save re-spending.

Many mothers allow their children to pick at their food and leave it on their plate without teaching them to eat what is in front of them. Good food is thrown in the trash. This is wasteful.

May God deliver us from being in the "foolish women category."

Prayer:
"Father, please touch my lips with coals from off the altar. I don't want to speak negative words. Fill my mouth with encouraging and life-giving words that will build up my husband and my children. Amen."

Affirmation:
I'm building my home with uplifting words,
To do anything else is utterly absurd!

Day 74

Home Destroyers

Part 2b

"Poverty and shame shall be to him that refuseth instruction:
but he that regardeth reproof shall be honored"
(Proverbs 13:18).

Can you believe that there are more ways to pull down our home?

e) We pull down our home by not preparing for the future

As you read through Proverbs 31, you will notice that the virtuous woman did not live only for the present but prepared her home and household for whatever lay ahead.

Proverbs 31:27 says, *"She looks well to the ways of her household, and eats not the bread of idleness."* The words 'looks well' are translated from the Hebrew word *tsaphah*. It has two meanings:

To watch. It is the same word that is used for a watchman who watches over the city, e.g. Ezekiel 33:7. The wise woman is a watchwoman. She guards her home and her children's lives. She does not leave her post. She guards over what they see, hear, and read. She watches over her home to keep everything in order. She does not let things get out of control.

To lean forward, to peer into the distance. The wise woman does not think only about today, but about the future. She has food and necessities prepared in case of emergency. She has made strategies with her family so that they know what to do in a crisis. She is ready for whatever may happen.

Proverbs 31:18 says, *"Her lamp goes not out by night."* Now don't feel guilty; she is not working all night! Back in Bible days, they did not have electricity. Therefore, they kept a lamp burning, ready for any emergency. The dogs may bark at some intrusion or the baby could wake. She needed to keep the lamp ready to investigate or to minister to the needs of the baby or children. It could be catastrophic for a family to run out of oil for the lamp. The wise woman always made sure she had enough oil to keep the lamp burning continually.

Jesus told a story about this in Matthew 25:1-13. The wise virgins took not only their lamps but extra oil with them. The foolish didn't think of anything but the moment, and of course they ran out of oil! And they missed the coming of the bridegroom! What did Jesus call these women? You know. Foolish!

f) We pull down our home by being stubborn

Proverbs 1:7 says, *"Fools despise wisdom and instruction."* Read also Proverbs 1:22. The foolish woman thinks she knows it all and does not like to be corrected. The wise woman knows that she constantly needs correction from the Lord, from her husband, and others, in order to keep learning and walking in the ways of the Lord. I don't always like it when my husband corrects me, but I know it keeps me on the right track. I want to receive correction and wisdom from others because I don't want to stay the same. I still have so much changing and learning to do. I want to have a soft heart to hear what God tells me.

The Scriptures tell us over and over again that it is the wise who will receive instruction and correction. The word that is used continually is "hear." Hear instruction. Hear counsel. Listen to rebuke. The word "hear" is *shama* in the Hebrew. It means "to hear with attention or obedience, to give undivided listening attention." This should be our attitude toward correction and advice, rather than being reactionary. I notice that the word heart has a *t* added to hear. To have a heart that is soft and pliable, we have to have to hear what God wants to say to us, not only through His Word, but through other people speaking into our lives.

Much of what we do and think is conditioned by our deceived humanistic society. It is so much part of everything around us that we think it is normal. But the world's normal does not always match the Word of God. We must continually seek God and His Word for His truth. We must constantly check to seek if we are lining up with His plan for motherhood and family life.

I have had to change and repent about so many things over the years and I know that God still has so much to teach me. We must always be open to God's truth. Read the beautiful family Psalms (Psalm 127 and 128) every week. They will keep you in line with God's heart for families rather than the humanistic thinking of this world.

Sometimes we have to humble our ears to hear counsel. Proverbs 22:17 says, *"**Bow down thine ear, and hear** the words of the wise, and apply thine heart unto my knowledge."*

We need to take notice of Proverbs 8:33, *"**Hear** instruction, and be wise, and refuse it not."* Also Proverbs 15:32, *"He that refuses instruction despises his own soul: but he that **hears** reproof gets understanding."*

g) We pull down our home by being loud and brash

Proverbs 9:13 says, *"The foolish woman is clamorous: she is simple, and knoweth nothing."* Isn't it an ugly sight to see a mother shouting brazenly at her children? This picture is the opposite of a wise woman who builds up her home.

"Her voice was ever soft, gentle and low, an excellent thing in a woman."
~ William Shakespeare

Prayer:

"Lord, please give me a hearing heart that is open to correction. I know that as I am open to correction, my children will be more open to correction too. Thank you, Lord. Amen."

Affirmation:

I'm a watchman in my home,
I will not vacate my post!
I'm open to wise correction
And filled with the Holy Ghost!

Further Study:

Go to page 215 to study more Scriptures about receiving instruction.

Home Destroyers

Part 3

"In the mouth of the foolish is a rod of pride"
(Proverbs 14:3).

What is the third tool that can pull down our home?

3. Pride

Proverbs 15:25 says, *"The Lord will destroy the house of the proud."* God hates pride. It is always destructive. Yet, how easily we succumb to this sin. Sometimes women feel ashamed if their house is poorer than their friends' homes. They want to keep up with the Joneses. They want their children to wear designer clothes. They want them to go to the best schools and best colleges. They want them to have degrees after their names. How are they going to do this?

Maybe they will be lured into the workforce to gain these aspirations. But the root of it all is pride. Instead of bringing blessing, it weakens home life. Children can enjoy a richer life and receive more blessings by having a contented mother in the home than wearing designer clothes and living in a fancier home.

Learning to be content is not easy but it is one of the godliest lessons we can teach our children. 1 Timothy 6:6 reminds us that, *"Godliness with contentment is great gain."* We definitely don't need all the things we think we need. We can live on a tenth of the stuff we think we need! Nor do our children need all the things they think they want. I am always challenged by the words in Nehemiah 9:20-21, *"You gave your good Spirit to instruct them, and did not withhold your manna from their mouth, and gave them water for their thirst. Forty years you sustained them in the wilderness, so that **they lacked nothing.**"* Read also Deuteronomy 8:3-4 and 29:5.

What did they have in the wilderness? God faithfully provided food and water and miraculously kept their clothes and shoes from wearing out. But, they lived in temporary tents. They had none of the modern conveniences that fill our homes today. They had no TVs. No running water or instant electricity. And yet God said **they lacked nothing.**

Proverbs 17:19 says, *"He that exalts his gate seeks destruction."* Matthew Henry comments on this Scripture: "He that exalts his gate, builds a stately house, at least a fine frontispiece, that he may outshine his neighbors, seeks his own destruction."

We know how Satan's pride wrought havoc and destruction in God's heavenly home. Isaiah 14:12-15 tells us that his pride not only caused him to be cast out of heaven but to become the one to *"weaken the nations."* Pride does not build up a home. It weakens a home and it tears it down.

May God help us to remember that each time we put on a proud look, speak prideful words and hold on to our stubbornness, we tear down our marriage and family a little more. Eventually we can destroy family relationships altogether.

Proverbs 16:18-19 says, *"Pride goes before destruction, and a haughty spirit before a fall. Better it is to be a humble spirit with the lowly, **than to divide the spoil with the proud.**"* Through divorce, many wives and husbands divide the spoil of their homes as their home folds up. The marriage is destroyed and consequently the children's lives are negatively affected—all because of pride! Too proud to say sorry. Too proud to ask for forgiveness. Too proud to take the humble attitude. Too proud to change. Pride is a bitter pill.

Pride is all about self! Humility is all about serving. Are we building up our home or tearing it down?

Prayer:
"Oh God, please show me the hideousness of pride in my life. Save me from tearing down my home because of my stubbornness and pride. Amen."

Affirmation:
I've decided to take the humble road,
It's the "blessing way" for my abode!

Further Study:
Go to page 217 to find more Scriptures about God's attitude to pride and humility.

Day 76

Home Destroyers

Part 4

"Do all things without murmurings and disputing: that ye may be blameless and harmless, the sons of God without rebuke, in the midst of a crooked and perverse nation, among whom ye shine as lights in the world"
(Philippians 2:14-15).

The following is one of the most destructive tools of the foolish woman.

4. Complaining

Psalm 106:25 says, *"They murmured in their tents, and hearkened not unto the voice of the Lord."* Read the story in Numbers chapter 14, especially verses 2 and 27.

Where were the people complaining? In their tents, which were their dwelling places in the wilderness. Where does most complaining happen? In the home. But what does it do? It tears down the home, whether we complain about our circumstances, the work we have to do, or our husband. Not only do the walls of our home hear it, but our children hear it. Worst of all, God hears it!

The children of Israel murmured and complained against Moses and Aaron, but when God heard it, He said they were complaining against Him. God says in Numbers 14:27, *"How long shall I bear with this evil congregation, which **murmur against Me**? I have heard the murmuring of the children of Israel, which they **murmur against Me**."* Help! When we murmur and complain about all our problems, God hears it as murmuring against Him.

The ten spies had returned from spying out the land of Canaan. It was a land flowing with milk and honey, but they complained about the fortified cities and the giants they would have to fight. It looked impossible! Even after all the miracles of coming out of Egypt and provision in the wilderness, they did not believe God could help them. They blamed Moses for bringing them out of Egypt. They complained that all their children would be taken as slaves.

What happened? God told them, *"Get back into the wilderness . . ."* He told them that they would all die in the wilderness and their children, who they complained would be taken as slaves, would be the ones to go into this magnificent land. Where do we end up when we complain? In the wilderness!

We take our families into
a wilderness journey when we complain!

The root of complaining is unbelief. *"Can God furnish a table in the wilderness?"* the Israelites cried out in unbelief (Psalm 78:19). "How could we ever have another baby?" you lament. "We can hardly make ends meet now!" "How can we afford to educate our children?" you ask in unbelief. "How can I put up with this little house any longer? I need more room," you complain. And so it goes on.

Here's a good habit to start.

Change every sigh into a Hallelujah!

Every time you are tempted to complain, turn your heart to the Lord and acknowledge that He is in control. "Thank you, Lord, I trust you. I know you are ordering my footsteps. I thank you that you are with me in these circumstances." It will take time to establish this new habit, but keep at it.

It doesn't mean that your circumstances will necessarily change, but you will change. God promises in Isaiah 43:1-3 that when you pass through the waters, *"I will be with you. They will not overflow you."* God says that when you go through the fire, *"You will not be burned, neither shall the flame kindle upon you."*

What is your confession? "I'm going through a fiery trial. I don't know how I can make it." Or, "Thank you, Lord, no matter how hot it gets, I will not be burned because you are with me!"

When I complained as a young child, my mother would immediately direct me to think about those who were poor and suffering in the world and didn't have all the blessings that I enjoyed. There are millions in the world who live in abject poverty, without running water, adequate food, shelter, or any of the basic amenities of life which we are accustomed to. My husband, who has ministered in the slums of India and many third world countries, often says, "Just to live in a tent in America makes you a millionaire!"

The Karen people, the displaced people of Burma, have been fighting for their survival for over 50 years in a genocidal war against them from the Burmese government. We complain about keeping up with homeschooling. The Karen try to school their children while they live in hiding. We complain when things are not going the way we want when we give birth. Many Karen mothers give birth while running from the enemy. No time for recovery. No time for relaxing with their baby. No gifts. No excited calls from family and friends.

The wife of the founder of the *"Free Burma Rangers"* (an adventurous and brave team who seek to help these displaced people) shares about the love, forgiveness and generosity of the Karen, even in the midst of suffering and hardship. She says, "The gifts they gave were of themselves—their time, energy and love. In my experience in the West it is easier to go to the store and buy a trinket as a gift. For this reason I have chosen to raise my children in this war. The influence of these people is something I have never experienced anywhere else."

Prayer:
"Oh Lord, I find it so easy to complain. Please give me strength to create a new habit of praising instead of protesting, gladdening others instead of grumbling, and being content instead of complaining. Amen."

Affirmation:
"Not for the lip of praise alone,
Nor e'en the praising heart
I ask, but for a life made up
Of praise in every part!"
~ Horatius Bonar

Home Destroyers

Part 5

"He that is soon angry dealeth foolishly"
(Proverbs 14:17).

"Be not hasty in thy spirit to be angry: for anger rests in the bosom of fools"
(Ecclesiastes 7.9).

Today we look at the last of the seven tools that can pull down our marriage and home.

5. Contention

Proverbs 19:13, *"The contentions of a wife are a continual dropping."* This is repeated again in Proverbs 27:15. In fact, Proverbs 27:16 continues, *"He who would restrain her restrains the wind, and grasps oil with his right hand."*

Proverbs 21:19 says, *"It is better to dwell in the wilderness, than with a contentious and an angry woman."* This is also repeated again in Proverbs 21:9 and 25:24.

Other versions of the Bible translate this contentious woman as "crabby, complaining, nagging, quarrelsome, ill-tempered, cross and petulant, scolding and irritable." The actual Hebrew word is *madown* which means "to quarrel, to cause discord or strife." Not a very nice description, is it?

It's easy to nag. It's easy to pick a quarrel. But it is destructive, so why do we do it?

Does this mean that we cannot tell our husband something that we are concerned about? No. We are **workers together** in building our family. Share your concerns with your husband in a spirit of meekness. Ask him how he thinks the situation could be remedied. Men love to give answers.

Once you have shared your concerns, keep quiet. But here's the secret. You don't keep quiet on your knees. Cry out to God and ask Him to deal with your husband. Don't give up praying until you see the answers.

The opposite of contention is harmony and unity. What can you do next time you feel contentious? Say No to your fleshly feelings and by faith speak harmonious words. You won't feel like it. You'd much rather nag or start a quarrel, but that's your old nature to which you are still accustomed. Instead, remember that the Holy Spirit indwells you. Turn to Him and ask Him to reveal His Spirit of harmony and peace-making through you.

6. Adultery

Proverbs 2:16-18 says, *"To deliver you from the immoral woman, from the seductress who flatters with her words, who forsakes the companion of her youth, and forgets the covenant of her God. For her house leads down to death, and her paths to the dead."* Read also Proverbs 7:27.

Adultery not only destroys the marriage but the children too. When God talks about the breaking up of the covenant of marriage in Malachi 2:13-16, He uses the words *"violence"* and *"treacherously."* In fact, in this short passage he repeats the word "treacherously" three times! God sees the breaking up of the marriage through adultery as **treacherous**! The Hebrew word is *bagad* and means "traitorous, unfaithful, deceitful, and also implies pillage." Read Jeremiah 3:20.

How can it be that adultery is prevalent in the church today? I remember growing up in a little town in New Zealand. If a husband or wife went off with someone else, it was the disgust of the town. And that was the attitude of non-Christians! Yet now it is prevalent for Christians to show tolerance for something God calls treacherous!

7. Rendering evil for good

Proverbs 17:13, *"Whoso rewards evil for good, evil shall not depart from his house."*

How important it is to show a grateful heart to those who have blessed us in our lives. We can take things for granted so easily, can't we? It's easy to carry on with life and forget the goodness of others. There are times when people speak evil about those who have blessed them. We have experienced this many times in our lives. But we dare not get bitter. We must keep on blessing them and trust God to work in their lives. And God does not forget. God does His own avenging in His own time and in His own way. We can leave these situations totally with God.

Romans 12:19-21 says, *"Dearly beloved, avenge not yourselves . . . for it is written, Vengeance is mine; I will repay, saith the Lord. Therefore if thine enemy hunger, feed him; if he thirst, give him drink: for in so doing thou shalt heap coals of fire on his head. Be not overcome of evil, but overcome evil with good."* Read Proverbs 25:21-22 and Romans 12:20.

Prayer:

"Oh God, please save me from being cranky and contentious. Please convict me when I become irritable or quarrelsome. Fill me with your Holy Spirit and help me establish unity in my home. Amen."

Affirmation:

I've had enough of being crabby,
I'm changing now to being happy!

Is Your Home a Lighthouse?

"All the children of Israel had light in their dwellings"
(Exodus 10:23).

One of the greatest challenges I faced in raising our children was when we left the shores of our little country of New Zealand to live on the Gold Coast of Australia. My husband's mission was to pioneer a church in that place and we pastored there for nearly 10 years. Our home looked out on Jupiter's Casino. Our church was also opposite this gambling place. The Gold Coast is a tourist area and playground for all kinds of sin and seduction. When we moved there, most of our children were in their teens, the most vulnerable age. I cried out to God, "Oh Father, please help me to keep our children pure in the midst of all this evil."

God's grace was upon us. Instead of being on the defensive, our children were on the offensive. They totally involved themselves with us in the church life. They began to preach in the open air mall in the heart of Surfers Paradise. When Rocky was only 13 years, hundreds would gather around to hear this young guy, preaching with bare-feet and jeans.

Our home burst to the seams with young people. As they sang the songs of Zion with all their hearts, the music reverberated down the canal! Soon the complaints started coming and we were ordered to stop or be evicted from our home. The neighbors didn't mind the drug houses on the same street but were offended at hearing gospel songs. The media heard about it and the reporters arrived. The headlines in the paper displayed, *"No to Hymns, Yes, to Hookers."*

A lighthouse is not set in a beautiful park. Lighthouses are built in the most dangerous and ferocious places to warn ships of danger. Our homes should be a sanctuary from the world where our children can grow strong and pure in the Lord, but they should also be lighthouses, beaming forth God's love, truth, and light to the community, When Jesus came into a home in Capernaum, *"it was noised that he was in the house"* (Mark 2:1). Are the neighbors around you aware that Jesus lives in your home?

We now live out in the woods of Tennessee, USA, but we are still not exempt from evil. In this tranquil place of God's earth, a man was recently charged with raping an old woman on a nearby road. Drug dealers live around. There will always be the darkness of sin around us, but we are here to shine light into the darkness (Matthew 5:14-16 and Philippians 2:15-16). The more evil encroaches upon us, the more we must shine! Paul encourages us in Philippians 2:14-16 to *"shine as lights"* in the midst of a *"crooked and perverse nation."*

Isaiah 60:1-3 states, *"Arise, shine; for thy light is come, and the glory of the Lord is risen upon thee. For, behold, the darkness shall cover the earth, and gross darkness the people: but the Lord shall arise upon thee, and his glory shall be seen upon thee."* Read also Matthew 5:14-16.

There was darkness in the homes of all the Egyptians, but light in the dwellings of God's people. Do people around see the light shining from your home? Do they see your committed marriage and your love for one another? Are they aware of the joy, fun, and laughter that emanates from your home? Do they see you sharing your home and your meals with others? Would they come to you when in need because they know you have the answers?

Prayer:
Dear Father, please fill our home with your light. Help us to be a lighthouse, showing your love and truth to many other families.

Affirmation:
The darker the night, the brighter we shine!

You Gotta Learn to Wait!

*"Therefore will the Lord wait, that He may be gracious unto you,
and therefore will he be exalted, that he may have mercy upon you:
for the Lord is a God of judgment: blessed are all they that wait for him"*
(Isaiah 30:18).

Can I let you in on a little secret? To walk with God you will need to learn how to wait. God is a God who waits! He waits to answer our prayers. He waits to be gracious to us. He waits for His right time to bring deliverance to us.

But, do we like waiting? No way. We want our prayers answered immediately. We want things to work out the way we want them right now. We are impatient because we live in time. But, God doesn't live in time. He lives in the eternal world. He governs the world from an eternal perspective. He watches over our lives from the eternal realm. And He knows what He is doing. He has everything in control. He is never too early and never a day too late.

Because God is a Father, He shows His father heart to us when we are first born into His family. When we become believers, we are born again into the family of God and are little babes in Christ. God ministers to us as a baby. He meets all our needs and answers all our prayers in the same way we constantly minister to the needs of our little nursing baby.

However, we would be distraught if our little baby didn't grow up and learn to do things for himself. As our children grow older, we don't continue to run to their every need. God also wants us to grow and mature. He wants our faith to be purified. He wants us to learn to trust and love Him, not for what He does for us but for who He is.

Do you want to grow and mature in your faith? Learn to wait. Deliberately quieten your restless heart and wait for Him. Trust Him. He hasn't forgotten you. He longs to be gracious to you and show you His compassion, but He knows that you will grow stronger and more mature as you learn to wait. If you keep jumping up and down and demanding God to do what you want Him to do immediately, you are still in the baby stage.

Wait for God to bring His answers to you. Often we don't receive God's answer because we don't wait long enough. Wait for God's provision. When you need something, don't rush out and buy it immediately. Give God time to show His provision. You will be amazed at how God will provide if you give Him time!

How should you wait?

1. Patiently

Psalm 37:7 says, *"Rest in the Lord and **wait patiently** for Him."* This is only a little Scripture, but if you put it into practice, it will work wonders in your life. You might like to write it out and pin it up where you can see it all through the day. You might like to make it a memory verse for the whole family.

2. Quietly

Lamentations 3:26 says, *"It is **good** that one should hope and **wait quietly** for the salvation of the Lord."* As you learn to wait, it will bring a rest to your soul—and your home. Also, as your children observe your example, they too will learn how to wait. This is an experience that many modern day children have never learned. They are used to getting whatever they want when they want it. In doing so, they don't experience the "expectation of waiting." They miss out on the "wonder" of this feeling.

As a child, I remember the longing and anticipation I felt as we waited from one Christmas to the next to receive our Christmas gifts. We didn't get things through the year and Christmas was the time we received gifts from our parents and loved ones. As a child it seemed an eternity to wait from one Christmas to the next. The anticipation was hardly bearable. But it made the receiving of the gifts incredibly exciting. The joy was heightened and intensified because of the anticipation and waiting.

3. Expectantly

The Bible talks about the expectation of waiting. Psalm 62:5 says, *"My soul, wait thou only upon God; for my **expectation** is from Him."* Waiting is good for the soul and good for the character.

There are two different aspects to waiting: waiting for God and waiting on God. We have talked about waiting for God. What about waiting on God? I believe this means to look up to the Lord in every circumstance of our life and each moment of the day. Instead of looking at the problem, look up to the Lord in expectation. Keep your eyes upon Him. Rely on Him, not on your own judgment or intelligence. How often should we do this?

a) All day long!

Psalm 25:5, *"On thee do I wait **all the day**."*

b) Continually!

Hosea 12:6, *"Wait on thy God **continually**."*

It's a lifestyle of waiting on the Lord. Would you like to start making this a habit of your life? Look at all the blessings you will receive as you live this lifestyle.

1. You will not be ashamed. God will never let you down (Psalm 25:3 and Isaiah 49:23).
2. You will inherit the earth (Psalm 37:9).
3. You will be blessed (Isaiah 30:18).
4. God will strengthen your heart (Psalm 27:14).
5. God will be your help and shield (Psalm 33:20).
6. God will save you (Proverbs 20:22 and Isaiah 25:9).
7. God will renew your strength (Isaiah 40:31).
8. God will be good to you (Lamentations 3:25).

And you've just got to read Isaiah 64:4, *"For since the beginning of the world men have not heard, nor perceived by the ear, neither hath the eye seen, O God, beside thee, what he hath prepared for him that waiteth for him."*

May you be a woman who knows how to wait.

Prayer:

"Lord, teach me how to wait on you. Help me to quietly wait in patience for your perfect answer. Save me from aborting what you want to do in my life and the life of my family because of my impatience. Amen."

Affirmation:

I'm learning to trust God more and more as I wait for His answer.

Day 80

Lasting Treasures

"Do not lay up for yourselves treasures on earth, where moth and rust destroy and where thieves break in and steal; but lay up for yourselves treasures in heaven, where neither moth nor rust destroys and where thieves do not break in and steal. For where your treasure is, there your heart will be also" (Matthew 6:19-21).

I received a phone call from an *Above Rubies* reader. "God has visited us," she told me with excitement. She was bursting with the news of the conception of their tenth baby! It was her seventh conception after a reversal.

As we chatted together, she shared how she and her husband felt sorry for their friends They and their friends had all sterilized about the same time after having two or three children. After being convicted of the Lord, this couple got a reversal, but their friends stayed sterilized! When they meet up with them, from time to time, they notice the boringness of their lives. Their children have grown up and they have to find things to fill their uninteresting lives. The wives go out to work each day and need to find entertainment to fill their lives for the rest of the time.

"But, our lives are so full," she exclaimed. "We have six extra precious children filling our home, children that we may never have had if God hadn't revealed to us the error of our ways. We are filled with joy every day. We are never bored. Our lives are full and complete. God is so good."

This mother is not only filled with joy, she is employed full-time by God. She is doing a lasting work. She is involved in an eternal mission to mold her children for heaven. She is not deceived by the things of this world that will one day pass away.

Another mother and teen daughter visited me some time ago. The mother had stopped at two children, but later her husband had a reversal from his vasectomy and now God has blessed them with five more wonderful children. As the 18-year old daughter held the youngest baby, she exclaimed, "We were such a boring family before we had these children. Now we are constantly laughing at the things they do and say."

A young mother shared with me recently how many of her friends waited a number of years before having children after they married. Now that they have their "two" children, they constantly talk of the fun they had before they had children and can't wait for their children to be off their hands so they can enjoy their own pleasures again.

Unfortunately, this attitude subconsciously tells the children they are a nuisance. This, in turn, affects their behavior so they become difficult to handle. Because they have more behavior problems, the parents begin to dislike parenting and want to vacate the home more than ever. It is a vicious circle.

On the other hand, I think of a lovely family of seven children who stayed in our home. The children were well trained and beautifully behaved. Each morning the mother would get up and exclaim, "How come I am so blessed to be the mother of these children?" She is awed at the privilege of being their mother.

You cannot find satisfaction and freedom by being released from your tedious circumstances. You cannot find true freedom by making sure you cannot have any more children. You may be free of more children, but other things in life will dominate you instead.

You can fill your life and your home with precious gifts from God. Or you can fill your life with your own interests and career. You can invest in material pursuits and temporal pleasures. I'm sure you will enjoy yourself but it will only be for this life. Every temporal thing we invest in will one day be forgotten. Every material possession we spend time acquiring will be left behind. However, children will live forever. They are lasting possessions.

Why not fill your life with the lasting treasures?

Prayer:

"Oh God, show me what is real and lasting. Please lead me back to your way when my life gets entangled with the things of this world. Lead me back to the true riches. Amen."

Affirmation:

I am investing my life in that which will last forever!

172

Leaning on Jesus

"Who is this that cometh up from the wilderness, leaning upon her beloved?"
(Song of Solomon 8:5).

The Song of Solomon is a very precious book of the Bible. It is a beautiful picture of marriage and it is also a picture of Christ and His bride.

The above Scripture also reveals the journey of Israel in the wilderness. She went into the wilderness with an independent spirit, full of doubts, murmurings, and complainings against the Lord. At the end of 40 years she eventually comes forth dependent upon God.

Although we are born dependent (Psalm 22:10), reliant upon our mother's breasts, it doesn't take long before the independent spirit takes over. The spirit of this age programs women to be independent. They are taught in school and college to be independent. They are warned that marriage may not work and, therefore, they must prepare for an independent lifestyle. To rely on a husband is considered weakness. But, independence is a trait of the flesh. It does not belong to the kingdom of God. It was independence and pride that caused Satan to be cast out of heaven (Isaiah 14:12-15).

The Word of God continually warns us about relying on our own self-sufficiency. Instead, we are encouraged over and over again to trust in the Lord and to lean upon Him.

Proverbs 3:5-6 says, *"Trust in the Lord with all thine heart; and lean not unto thine own understanding. In all thy ways acknowledge Him, and He shall direct thy paths."*

Our ability and understanding is flimsy. When we lean upon it, it will bend and often break beneath us. Also, when we lean to our own understanding, we usually lean to what suits us. We lean toward selfishness. We lean towards the easy way out. We may think that "my way" is the best, but it may not be the best decision in the long term. God's ways, even though contrary to everything we want to do, always lead to ultimate blessing.

No wonder Proverbs 28:26 says, *"He that trusts in his own heart is a fool."* Isaiah 36:6 tells us that when we lean upon Egypt (which is a type of the world's wisdom), it will go into the hand and pierce it.

Isaiah 30:1-3 says, *"Woe to the rebellious children, saith the Lord, that take counsel, but not of me . . . that walk to go down into Egypt and have not asked at my mouth; to strengthen themselves in the strength of Pharaoh, and to trust in the* shadow of Egypt! Therefore shall the strength of Pharaoh be your shame, and the trust in the shadow of Egypt your confusion."

Isaiah 31:1-3 gives a similar warning, "Woe to them that go down to Egypt for help; and stay on horses, and trust in chariots, because they are many, and in horsemen, because they are very strong; but they look not unto the Holy One of Israel, neither seek the Lord!"

When we lean upon our God, He will never fail us. We can lean hard. We can put our whole weight upon Him and He will not move. He is our Rock. He is our Fortress. He is our Buckler. We cannot fall for underneath are the everlasting arms (Deuteronomy 33:27).

Get into the habit of leaning. It is not weakness. It is the true spirit of marriage and a picture of the bride of Christ leaning upon her Beloved. It is true spirit of our relationship with the Lord.

The word "lean" in the Hebrew is *sha-an* which depicts an attitude of trust and ultimate dependence. This same word is translated by other words in the King James Bible:

2 Chronicles 13:18, "The children of Judah prevailed, because they **relied** (sha-an) upon the Lord God of their fathers."

2 Chronicles 14:11, "And Asa cried unto the Lord his God, and said, Lord, it is nothing with thee to help, whether with many, or with them that have no power: help us, O Lord our God; for we **rest** (sha-an) on Thee, and in Thy name we go against this multitude."

Isaiah 50:10, "Let him trust in the name of the Lord, and **stay** (sha-an) upon his God." Read also Isaiah 10:20.

Dear mother, why not try leaning upon the Lord today rather than trying to do everything in your own strength. It is not weakness, but ultimate maturity.

Prayer:

"Dear Heavenly Father, I repent of my independent spirit and wanting to do things my way. I repent of my independence in my marriage. I repent of 'going down to Egypt' and leaning on the counsel of this world. I know that when I lean upon my own resources, I fail. Please teach me to lean upon you moment by moment. Amen."

Affirmation:

"Leaning, leaning,
Safe and secure from all alarms;
Leaning, leaning,
Leaning on the everlasting arms."
~ Elisha A. Hoffman

Day 82

The Comforts of Sterility

*"For whosoever will save his life shall lose it:
and whosoever will lose his life for my sake shall find it"*
(Matthew 16:25).

Recently I read a phrase that captivated my attention. In his book *"Caesar and Christ,"* Will Durant states that one of the reasons for the fall of the Roman Empire was that they sacrificed their civilization for "the comforts of sterility."

Yes, there are comforts to sterility. No sleepless nights. No sacrifice. Freedom to pursue your career. Time for pleasure. Make more money. Get a bigger house, better car, and higher status symbol. But, what's the end result of choosing sterility? Sadness. Loneliness. Emptiness. And eventually the decline of a civilization.

Our culture, out of the church and in the church, is rooted in pleasure seeking. We are shallow, selfish, and want to do our own thing. But, nothing comes of a fruitless vine. It is useless. Good for nothing. It doesn't provide food or blessing for anyone.

This is not what life is all about. Life is sacrifice. In fact, you can't have life without death. What did Jesus say in John 12:24? *"Except a corn of wheat fall into the ground and die, it abideth alone, but if it die, it bringeth forth much fruit."* When we live for ourselves, we lose our life. When we lay down our life in daily sacrifice we find it. This is an eternal law.

What is the opposite to "the comforts of sterility?" It would have to be "the sacrifices of fertility." I have to concede that there are sacrifices to fertility. You will have to lay down your own life. You will have sleepless nights. You will have burdens to bear. But, oh the joys, the fruitfulness, and the rewards! You will reap the fruit of your labor and sacrifice. You will rejoice in godly offspring who will take God's love and salvation to the nations of the world. You will fill the world with more of God's light and truth because of the godly "arrows" you are daily sharpening and polishing. Your life will not end in loneliness, but you will be surrounded with children and grandchildren.

You are also part of building and prospering your nation. Every child you bring into the world is not only one life, but also the beginning of another dynasty. Every child you refuse to bring into the world is not only one life that is denied, but also a whole dynasty that is lost to the world and the generations to come!

175

We are unknowingly driving down a road to destruction. The average number of children per family in USA is 1.8. The Islamic people are multiplying at an average of 6.8 per family. Islam is the fastest growing religion in the world today without evangelizing, but multiplying only.

To multiply is the secret to take dominion. We see this principle in the very first words that man ever heard from the mouth of God. We read in Genesis 1:28, *"God blessed them, and God said unto them, 'Be fruitful, and multiply, and replenish the earth, and subdue it: and have dominion."* If we want to take dominion for the kingdom of God on the earth, we must multiply. If we want our nation to continue, we have to multiply. When we stop multiplying, we lose ground. We diminish. Eventually we disappear from the horizon.

God wants His people who belong to His kingdom to fill the earth with His salvation and glory. Our purpose is not to just hold the fort until Jesus comes, but to be invaders! We are the children of light, invading the darkness with the light of Jesus. We are truth bearers, exposing the deceptions of this humanistic age. We are the rivers of the pure water of God's throne, ministering life and healing to a sick and hurting world. We are dying to ourselves to bring forth much fruit. We are choosing and embracing life instead of death and filling the world with the godly seed. We are not here to retreat, but to subdue and invade.

This is what God's people did when they were in Egypt. They became a threat to the Egyptians because they grew *"more and mightier"* than them. Are we, the people of God, a threat to the heathen? We can be if we have the testimony of God's people in Egypt who *"were fruitful, and increased abundantly, and multiplied, and waxed exceeding mighty; and the land was filled with them"* Exodus 1:7-9. Read also Psalm 80:8-11.

Prayer:

"Oh God, I am sorry that I have been deceived. I repent of my selfishness. I repent of holding back the godly seed. Please give me an invading mentality. Help me to see your purposes and vision. Please save me from my selfishness. Amen."

Affirmation:

I am helping to prepare an army of invaders who will fill the land with God's glory.

Day 83

Which Language Do You Speak?

"He that comes from above is above all; he who is of the earth is earthly and speaks of the earth"
(John 3:31).

When folks came to my 60th birthday, they were given a questionnaire to fill in regarding information about my life. One of the questions was, "How many languages does she speak?" It was a trick question, because I have to confess, to my shame, that I only speak English. If I could live my life over again, I would change that. I feel ashamed when I travel to other countries and mix with people who speak three or four languages. I remember staying with a family in Malaysia. Between them, the husband and wife spoke more than six languages in which they constantly talked to their children. Consequently, their young children fluently spoke six languages.

However, more important than speaking many languages, is that we speak the *right* language! There are thousands of languages and dialects in the world, but there are only two categories to which they all belong—the language of earth and the language of heaven!

There is a vernacular that belongs to the kingdom of Satan and a completely different one that belongs to the kingdom of God.

When we are born again into the kingdom of God, we must learn the language of this new kingdom. It is a language of love and purity. It is a language of truth. It confesses the truth of God's principles, even if it is the opposite to how we feel. It speaks divine truth, even if it is opposite to what the rest of the world is saying. It aligns with God.

Now please don't get me wrong. I'm not talking about speaking religious-sounding words that don't relate to life. They are phony. They are religious, but not reality.

God's language is real. It is part of the nitty-gritty of life. It speaks truth, in plain words, in the midst of humanistic deception. It speaks wisdom in the midst of man's foolishness. It talks love in the midst of hate. It retaliates with blessing when abused, persecuted, and mistreated. It rings with praises to the Lord instead of groaning and grumbling. It talks faith in the midst of doubt and delusion.

We don't learn to speak this language immediately. It takes time because it is totally opposite to the way we used to speak. We have to practice it. It will not feel natural at first, but we keep speaking it in faith until it becomes normal.

Philippians 3:20 says, *"Our citizenship is in heaven, from which we also eagerly wait for the Saviour, the Lord Jesus Christ."* Citizens of heaven will speak the language of heaven.

As Jews from all over the world make *aliyah* to Israel, they immediately go to an Ulpan to learn Hebrew, the language of their new country. It is mandatory. Our daughter, Evangeline, had the privilege of attending an Ulpan when she lived in Israel.

We have had to learn many new words since coming from New Zealand to live in America. We used to say "nappies" but now we say "diapers." We used to say "dummy" but now we say "pacifier." We used to say "pushchair" but now we say "stroller." Instead of talking about the "boot" of a car, we now call it the "trunk." And so it goes on and on. Bill Bryson in his book, *Mother Tongue* says that there are some 40,000 words that are different in American English to British English. I can believe it.

Which language are you speaking? Are you still speaking the old language that belongs to Satan's kingdom, the lingo of doubt, defeat, dread, and deception? Or, do you speak the language of your citizenship which are words of love, joy, peace, praise, and faith?

1 John 4:5-6 says, *"They are of the world. Therefore **they speak as of the world**, and the world hears them. We are of God: He who knows God hears us: he who is not of God does not hear us. By this we know the spirit of truth and the spirit of error."*

Make it your aim to become fluent in your new language, the language of heaven. Your speech will expose to which kingdom you belong.

Prayer:

"Oh God, please touch my lips with your heavenly fire. Cleanse my lips. Purify my speech. Teach me your language. Lord, I belong to a heavenly country. Help me to speak the language of this country. Amen."

Affirmation:

I am practicing my heavenly language each day.

Day 84

Your Testimony

*"Let your light so shine before men, that they may see your good works,
and glorify your Father which is in heaven"*
(Matthew 5:16).

One time when Evangeline (our daughter, a mother of 10 children), was in a Wal-Mart with five of her little ones, a lady came up to her and said, "I have to tell you that you are an incredible mother. Here's $10.00!"

Evangeline continued her shopping in Wal-Mart, but about ten minutes later this same lady came up to her again and said, "I'm not done. I have to tell you again that you are a wonderful mother. Here's another $10.00!"

Wherever we go, people are watching. We can be a light, shining God's truth brightly to those we meet, or we can show a blurred and distorted picture of God's plan for us. I believe the greatest testimony a mother can give to the world is to be a joyful and contented mother of children. Psalm 113:9 talks of *"the joyful mother of children."*

When you go out with your children, lift your head high, put a smile on your face, and be proud to be a mother. You have the most important career in the nation. God Himself is your employer and you are determining the future of this nation.

Be a light in the midst of a society that does not embrace children. Do not be intimidated. Show your love for your children as you speak sweetly to them and are patient with them. If God has blessed you with a number of children, be proud of your "blessings" from the Lord. You will reveal to the world what God is like for He loves children. Jesus did not reject children. He welcomed the children to come to Him.

Mark 9:36-37 says, *"And he took a child, and set him in the midst of them and when he had taken him in his arms, he said unto them, whosoever shall receive one of such children in My name, receives Me; and whosoever shall receive Me, receives not Me, but Him that sent Me."*

There is no more beautiful picture than to see a serene and happy mother with well-trained children in tow. There can be no argument from those who don't embrace children.

I believe we should not only be happy about our own children, but all children. When you see a mother with a baby, take notice of her baby and encourage her.

I think of my husband's father. He fathered nine of his own children, but he loved all children. He could not go down the street without stopping every mother with children. He would talk to the children and especially ooh and aah at the baby. He loved babies. He went to be with the Lord many years ago, but one Christmas our daughter, Serene, painted a picture of him for my husband. Underneath she wrote the caption, *"Jack Hedley Campbell—Lover of children."* What a testimony to have over our lives. It is the same testimony God has.

Let the world see you are a *"joyful mother of children."*

Prayer:
"Lord, please help me to be a shining mother, shining with the light of your joy in my home and when I walk down the street with my children. Amen."

Affirmation:
I am proud to be called a mother.

Godly Children?

"Has not the one God made and sustained for us the spirit of life?
And what does he desire? Godly offspring. So take heed to yourselves
and let none be faithless to the wife of his youth. For I hate divorce,
says the Lord the God of Israel"
(Malachi 2:15 RSV).

God reveals His heart about marriage in the above Scripture. He wants the wife and husband to be one. He wants them to be faithful to one another, not divorced. He makes His reason for saying this very clear. The disruption of marriage tampers with the godly offspring. What God looks for in marriage more than anything else is godly children. This is His heart's desire. He looks eagerly for the coming children. This is His plan for marriage.

It is the nature of God to want children in His image. And because we were made in the likeness and image of God, it is inherent for us to also want children in our image. We long to see who they will be like, more like the father, or more like the mother.

And yet, we now live in a distorted age. Couples have been so brainwashed by humanist deception that they often refuse to have children, or at least limit how many they have. They live counter-culture to God's kingdom and to their own instinctive design. Grandparents wait to continue the godly dynasty. While they live to their own desires, God waits with patience to see children born in His image. Each new precious baby is created in the image of God and He wants His image multiplied in the earth.

Even more challenging is that it is not just offspring for which God looks. It is **godly** offspring. The margin in my Bible says, *"the seed of God."* What kind of children are the seed of God? It is even more challenging when we find that the Hebrew word is *elohim*. The name, Elohim, is one of the names of God, the first name by which God introduces himself to us in Genesis 1:1. Elohim occurs 2,570 times in the Bible.

Elohim is used 35 times in Genesis 1:1 to 2:4 revealing God's creative and governing power. He created this vast universe by His spoken word. Elohim is the one who brought "cosmos out of chaos, light out of darkness, habitation out of desolation, and life in His image" (Nathan Stone). Because we are created in His image, we also have the ability to create. God has put into our mouths the power of the spoken word. We can minister life or death by our tongue (Proverbs 18:21). God wants us (and each new babe that is born) to create and speak for His kingdom and His glory. He wants the godly offspring to fill the earth with His words and truth.

Elohim also reveals God as a covenant keeping God. There are many Scriptures revealing this but here are a few:

Genesis 17:7, *"I will establish **my covenant between me and thee** and thy seed after thee in their generations for an **everlasting covenant**, to be a God (Elohim) unto thee, and to thy seed after thee."*

Genesis 9:15-17, *"And **I will remember my covenant** . . . And the bow shall be in the cloud; and I will look upon it, that I may remember the **everlasting covenant** between God (Elohim) and every living creature."*

On Joseph's death bed he said, *"God (Elohim) will surely visit you, and bring you out of this land unto the land which he **sware to Abraham, to Isaac, and to Jacob"*** (Genesis 50:24).

When Solomon dedicated the temple, he prayed, *"There is no God (Elohim) like thee, in heaven above, or on earth beneath, **who keepest covenant** and mercy with thy servants that walk before thee with all their heart"* (1 Kings 8:23).

Because Elohim is a covenant-keeping God. He wants us to also keep covenant. He wants each godly offspring to be a covenant-keeper. It is interesting that God talks about the godly seed coming forth in the context of a covenant keeping marriage. Malachi 2:14 RSV says, *"The Lord was witness to **the covenant between you and the wife of your youth**, to whom you have been faithless, though she is your companion and your wife by covenant."*

It is not having lots of children that will solve the world's problems. It is having **godly** children who will impact the nations for God. May God enable us to welcome the godly seed and train them to truly reveal the character of Elohim. Where could you find a more awesome career?

Prayer:

"Oh God, please help me to be a faithful covenant-keeper and to train my children to be the same. Amen."

Affirmation:

I have the awesome privilege to raise the "seed of God."

Day 86

I Need Strength!

"The Lord is the strength of my life"
(Psalm 27:1).

Ｗhat do you do when you run out of strength, as I am sure you often do? Where do you go?

Did you know that you have another resource when your strength wanes? Yes, it is in your God. He is your Strength. In fact, He is more than your strength. He is your EVERLASTING STRENGTH. His strength never runs out. It is inexhaustible. You can draw from it at any moment you wish. It is always available for you.

Isaiah 26:3-4, one of my favorite Scriptures says, *"Thou wilt keep him in perfect peace, whose mind is stayed on thee: because he trusts in thee. Trust ye in the Lord forever, for in the Lord Jehovah is EVERLASTING STRENGTH."*

I remember one time when our six children were little and I had many other things pressing upon me. I felt as though it was more than my strength could handle. Have you ever felt like that?

I awoke in the morning to have my Bible reading and prayer which is a habit of my life, and I poured out my inadequacies to the Lord. I was amazed! I could hardly believe that the words I read in 2 Corinthians 1:8-10 were exactly how I was feeling, *"For we would not, brethren, have you ignorant of our trouble which came to us in Asia, that we were **pressed out of measure, above strength**, insomuch that we despaired even of life."*

That was me! I was pressed out of measure. It was more than my strength could take, although I hadn't got to despairing of life!

What did Paul do when he was in this situation? I kept reading . . . *"But we had the sentence of death in ourselves, that **we should not trust in ourselves, but in God** which raised the dead. Who delivered us from so great a death, and doth deliver: **in whom we trust** that He will yet deliver us."*

At that moment, I saw the light. I realized that I was trusting in myself instead of His strength! Of course, my resources were not enough to carry me through. I repented. "I'm sorry, Lord," I cried, "I repent that I have been trusting in my own strength. I have forgotten to trust in your everlasting strength. I have forgotten that you are my Deliverer. I have forgotten that you are my Refuge. You are my Rock on whom I can lean. You are my Strength. I hand everything over to you. Thank you, Lord."

As I did this, a great peace swept over my soul. Although this was years ago, I can still remember that later in that day I tried to think of all those problems that were weighing me down. Can you believe it? I couldn't even think of one of them! It's amazing the difference that comes to us when we put our trust in the Lord instead of ourselves, isn't it? So many of our worries, depressions, fears, and frustrations are simply because we try to do it on our own and trust in our own strength.

God is waiting for us to rely on His strength. We will never be ashamed if we put our trust in the Lord. Don't try to carry all the burdens of the day yourself. Roll your burdens upon the Lord. He has promised to sustain you and His promises never fail.

He is the Strength of Your Life

I love Psalm 27:1 where David exclaims, "*The Lord is the strength of my life.*" What a wonderful confession. Why don't you make this your confession? Say these words out loud, right now. Say them again. And again. Receive the truth of them into your life.

Over and over again, David confesses that God is His strength. He didn't rely on his own strength, but trusted in God's unfailing strength. As you also continually make this confession, you will experience God's strength in your life. In fact, *"my Strength"* is one of the names that David and others in the Bible called God.

Psalm 18:1-2, "*I will love thee, O Lord, **my strength**.*" Read also Exodus 15:2; Psalm 19:14; 28:7; 31:4; 43:2; 46:1-3; 59:17; 62:7; 118:14; 144:1; Isaiah 12:2 and Habakkuk 3:19.

Psalm 18:32, "*It is God that girds me with strength.*"

Psalm 68:35, "*The God of Israel is he that gives strength and power unto his people.*"

He is the Strength of Your Heart

God is not only the strength of your life, but also the strength of your heart. When your heart fails for fear, God will strengthen you. When your heart is breaking, God will strengthen you. When your heart is sad and lonely, God will come to you.

Psalm 27:14, "*Wait on the Lord: be of good courage, and he shall **strengthen your heart**.*"

Psalm 31:24, "*Be of good courage, and he shall **strengthen your heart**, all ye that hope in the Lord.*"

Psalm 73:26, "*My flesh and my heart fails: but God is the **strength of my heart**, and my portion forever.*"

Isaiah 35:4, *"Say to them that are of a fearful heart, Be strong, fear not: behold, your God will come . . . He will come and save you."*

He is the Strength of Your Soul

Do you feel weak and spineless? God will make you strong on the inside so you will be able to stand against the wiles of the devil and the deceptions of society that are all around you.

Psalm 138:3, *"In the day when I cried thou answered me, and strengthened me with* **strength in my soul.***"*

Ephesians 3:16, *"That he would grant you, according to the riches of his glory, to be* **strengthened with might by his Spirit in the inner man.***"*

Make this your constant confession throughout this week. Continually speak these words out loud, *"The Lord is the strength of my life."*

Prayer:

"Lord, I confess that you are the strength of my life. Thank you for your strength that it is freely available to me moment by moment. I receive it and acknowledge it. I thank you that I can face all that I have to do today because of your inexhaustible and everlasting strength. Thank you in Jesus' name. Amen."

Affirmation:

I'm confessing it again . . . The Lord is the strength of my life!

Day 87

Enemy Chasers

"Five of you shall chase an hundred, and a hundred of you shall put ten thousand to flight: and your enemies shall fall before you by the sword" (Leviticus 26:8).

We can be a close-knit, loving family and yet live to ourselves. I believe we should lift up our eyes to see what an influence we can be as a family to the world. One of the greatest ways we can influence the world is by prayer. The power of praying families is enormous.

Prayer should be part of every home. Jesus said, *"My house shall be called a house of prayer"* (Luke 19:46). If our home belongs to the Lord, it will be a home of prayer. That means prayers will be conducted daily. That means prayer will happen spontaneously throughout the day. That means prayer will be very natural in our home. It will be as familiar as breathing to our children. As my husband often states, "If we haven't taught our children to pray, we haven't taught them."

One of the most powerful times in our home is our Family Devotions each evening where everyone prays around the table—father, mother, and all the children and whoever else happens to be at the table. We pray for current needs and the nation. Can you imagine the blessings that would come to us if every family prayed together each day for their nation?

We also pray for the nations of the world. It is amazing that we can sit around our dinner table in the Tennessee woods and yet see mighty things happen for God in countries of the world to which we have never visited.

Sometimes we encourage each one to pray for a country that is on their heart or comes to their mind. Currently we are using the book, *Praying Through the 100 Gateway Cities of the 10/40 Window*. After our Bible reading, we read the information about the city in the book and pray for that city for a week before going on to the next one. We certainly learn our geography as we pray for cities like El Aaiun in Western Sahara, Nouakchott in Mauritania, Ouagadougou in Burkina Faso, and Mogadishu in Somalia, etc. The children learn about the world, as they also learn to forget about themselves, and instead pray for needy, persecuted and often enslaved people.

God's Word tells us that five people can chase 100 aliens! How many children in your family? Do you have three! You, your husband and your children (five of you) you can put 100 enemies to flight! And think about this!

186

Only 20 families with five members can put 10,000 to flight! This is powerful! No wonder Satan seeks to get us interested in doing everything else but pray together as a family.

Dear mother, I know there are a thousand things that turn up to lure us away from this powerful ministry. Even "good things" keep us from this "best" task of moving the hand of God in prayer. Watch out for extra-curricular activities which keep you from this world-impacting ministry in your home. Prayer together doesn't just happen. You have to make it happen. You have to make it a commitment. But, you can do it. I have proved it over years and years and we are still doing it today.

As it comes to this culminating moment of the day when we have Family Devotions and pray together, I am aware of the power of what is happening. We are reaching out beyond our four walls. We are going into nations of the world that are closed to the Gospel. We are going into countries where we could be killed for preaching the Gospel—but we are going in by prayer. God hears our cries. He hears the cries of the children. He loves children's prayers.

The more people we have around our table, the more prayer goes up to the throne of grace. The more children you have praying around your table, the more impact you have upon the world. Praying together is the most important thing you can do together as a family.

The enemies of God will bite the dust as you and your family pray.

Prayer:

"Oh God, help me to never forget the power of prayer. Show me how I can get my family together every day to pray and impact the world. Amen."

Affirmation:

We are a missionary family, going into the countries of the world through the power of prayer!

Day 88

The Warmth of a Smile

"The Lord bless thee, and keep thee; The Lord make his face shine upon thee, and be gracious unto thee: The Lord lift up his countenance upon thee, and give thee peace"
(Numbers 6:24-26).

What a wonderful blessing to have God's face shine upon us and to bask in the favor of His smile. Both Knox and Moffat translate it this way, *"The Lord smile on thee."* God's blessing is His smile. It is the smile of His favor. It is the affirmation of His love to us. Let's read some other Scriptures from the Knox translation:

Psalm 21:6, *"Comforted by the **smile** of thy favor."*

Psalm 44:3, *"Thy **smile** shone upon them, in proof of thy favor."*

Psalm 67:1, *"May God be merciful to us, and bless us, may He grant us the favor of His **smile**."*

Psalm 80:3, 7, 19, *"**Smile** upon us, and we shall find deliverance."*

Psalm 90:17, *"The favor of the Lord our God **smile** upon us."*

Psalm 89:15, *"Happy is the people . . . that lives, Lord, in the **smile** of thy protection."*

Psalm 119:135, *"Restore to thy servant the **smile** of thy loving favor."*

Where do smiles come from? As with everything else, they originate in God. He smiled first before we smiled. He still smiles over us (Zephaniah 3:17).

A smile is like the sun shining upon us. There is one spot in the living area of our home where the sun shines in brightly. I love this spot. I gravitate to it. To bask in the warmth of the sun not only brings warmth to the physical body, but also to the soul. You can forget worries and problems when you bask in the sun.

Just as God blesses us with His smile, He wants us to bless our children in the same way. How often do you smile at your children? Occasionally? When they please you? Or do they bask in the warmth of your continual smiles? Smiling at your children will change the atmosphere of your home. It will change the attitudes and behavior of your children.

2 Corinthians 3:18 says, *"But we all, with open face beholding as in a glass the glory of the Lord, are changed into the same image from glory to glory, even as by the Spirit of the Lord."* The more we behold the Lord, the more we grow into His

likeness. In the same way, your children look at you all day. They reflect and act out what they see on your face. If you are always frowning at your children, expect to have unhappy and grumbling children. But, if you are always smiling at them, they will in turn become smiling happy children.

William Makepeace Thackeray said, "Mother is the name for God in the lips and hearts of little children." Are you showing the smile of God to your children?

They will thrive as they bask in the favor of your smile. Every time you smile at them, you tell them you love them, accept them, delight in them, and you are very glad God gave them to you. In the warmth of this blessing they will grow in grace and become all that God intends for them to be. All because of your smiles!

Why not try it? Start smiling today. Keep smiling at your children. Smile when you are happy. Smile when you are unhappy. Smile even when you don't feel like smiling.

By the way, when did you last smile at your husband? Really smile at him? Smiling will keep your marriage intact.

Prayer:

"Father, I thank you for the favor of your smile. Help me to pass on your blessing to my husband and children. Help me to be like you and smile. Amen."

Affirmation:

Today I will smile at my husband and children. I will bless them and bless myself.

Day 89

Faint, Yet Pursuing

"When Abram heard that his brother was taken captive, he armed his trained servants, born in his own house . . . pursued them . . . smote them, and pursued them . . . And he brought back all the goods, and also brought again his brother Lot, and his goods, and the women also, and the people"
(Genesis 14:14-16).

Abram must have been distraught when he heard that Lot was taken captive. But he didn't wallow in despair. Instead, he went into action. He got his household army together and pursued the enemy. They didn't give up until they smote them and recovered everyone and everything that had been taken.

Satan is our enemy who comes to rob, kill, and destroy. He is constantly out to rob us and sometimes he is successful. When this happens, what do you do? It is easy to throw up your hands in despair. But, don't let him win the victory. Go after him. Don't leave a stone unturned until you smite him and recover what you have lost!

Perhaps someone's marriage is breaking up in one of your family members. You want to cry. Do more than that. Ask God what you should do. I have a friend whose brother started having an affair with another woman. My friend was mad with the enemy who was seeking to destroy another marriage. She prayed of course. She got us all to pray. But, she also pursued the enemy. She took time out, and, with her mother, drove many hours to his city in an old "bomb" of a car, arriving in the evening. The next day she helped him to chop and stack wood and later that night she approached him. He told her to "butt out and mind her own business" otherwise he would never speak to her again.

"If that's the price I have to pay," replied his sister, "I will pay it. You brought your wife home for us to love and we have loved her. If you choose to leave her, we will support her and continue to love her. This affair is not love, but lust!"

Her words fell on deaf ears. She kept praying and God continued to work. A week later, his boss also talked to him and he came back to his wife. Her trip was worth it. Another defeat for the enemy who hates marriages!

A similar situation happened to David which you can read about in 1 Samuel 30. David came back from fighting to find his city of Ziklag burned to the ground. All the women and children were taken including David's two wives. David was greatly distressed. He and his men wept until they could weep no more. In fact, his men were so bitter they wanted to stone David.

But, David didn't stay in despair! He encouraged himself in the Lord His God. When he took his eyes off the terrible situation and looked to God, God was able to show him what to do. You can't hear from God when you are in the pit of sorrow. All you see and hear is desperation. But when you look to the Lord, He will give you strategy. He will show you a plan of attack against the enemy, just as he showed David.

Verses 9–17 tell us, *"So David went . . . David pursued, he and four hundred men . . . And David smote them from the twilight even unto the evening of the next day: and there escaped not a man of them, save four hundred young men, which rode upon camels, and fled."* It took more than one blow to defeat their enemy. They slaughtered them throughout the whole night and all the next day. They didn't give up until they recovered what they lost.

We read the victory in verses 18-19, *"And David recovered all that the Amalekites had carried away: and David rescued his two wives. And there was nothing lacking to them, neither small nor great, neither sons nor daughters, neither spoil, nor any thing that they had taken to them: David recovered all."*

I think it is time to recover what the enemy is stealing from God's people today. He robs marriages. He robs families. He robs parents of children. He even robs God of the godly seed that He wants to come forth to fulfill His purposes. There are many who sterilize to stop having God's children. They do it in ignorance, of course. "Isn't that what everyone does?" they say. Sadly, they don't realize that it is the enemy who robs them of life—a life that will live forever.

We should not allow the enemy to steal any longer. If a couple have sterilized, don't you think it would be a good idea to pursue a reversal? There will always be obstacles and financial challenges. Yet, while we do nothing, the devil laughs and holds up the flag of victory. It's time we pursued him until once again we hold the victory flag.

Has the enemy taken one of your children captive? Perhaps your situation is so sorrowful that you are still weeping. Of course you will weep. But don't weep forever. Encourage yourself in the Lord. Let Him show you what to do. And go after the enemy until you recover all. Even when you feel weak and helpless, keep on. Gideon was exhausted from chasing the enemy, but he kept on, *"faint, yet pursuing"* (Judges 8:4).

Prayer:

"Oh Lord God, please help me to be on watch against the enemy who comes to rob, kill, and destroy. When he robs me, give me strength to go on the attack and pursue the enemy. Amen."

Affirmation:

Even when weak, I will keep on pursuing!

Day 90

It's Futile!

*"Do not turn aside from following the Lord, but serve the Lord with all your heart. You must not turn aside, for then you would go after **futile** things which cannot profit or deliver, because they are futile"*
(1 Samuel 12:20-21 NASB).

When we turn away from the Lord, we tend to follow after futile things. When we keep close to the Lord, through prayer and guidance of His Word, He keeps our hearts in the right place and leads us into His truth. When we turn aside to our own ways, we have nothing to deter us from walking after vain things and running into deception.

Romans 1:18-28 tells us that when people turn aside from God and focus all their attention on themselves, worshipping *"the creature more than the Creator"*, they become *"futile in their speculations"* and God gives them over to a *"reprobate mind"* which is a mind that is void of all judgment and understanding.

We gain more understanding of the word "futile" (*tohu* in the Hebrew) by looking at other passages where it is used. We find that it also means . . .

Wasteful (Deuteronomy 32:10). To go a different way than God has planned for us is to waste our lives. I have always thought that the saddest thing anyone can do is to go through life doing their own thing and going their own way. They miss out on the destiny that God has planned for them before the foundation of the world. That's a wasted life.

Nothingness. Job 6:18 says, *"The paths of their way are turned aside: they go to nothing and perish."* There is only nothingness at the end of a life that is spent on itself. Luke 12:8-21 reveals the nothingness at the end for the one *"who lays up treasure for himself, and is not rich towards God."*

A Wilderness Experience (Deuteronomy 32:10 and Job 12:24). To turn aside from God's ways is always a wilderness experience.

Confusion (Isaiah 41:29). We live in a society that is deceived and deluded. Because we are engulfed by humanist thinking—in the media, the education system, and the mindset of the majority around is, it can seem normal to us. Unless we keep close to the Lord and live in His Word, we can also be deceived and confused without knowing it.

Vanity (Isaiah 40:17; 23; 44:9; 59:4). It is a vain thing to pursue our own way. It has no eternal reward.

Empty. The Jerusalem Bible and Complete Jewish Bible translate "tohu" as *empty*. Many people try to fill their lives with pleasure, satisfaction, and material possessions. They fill their homes with stuff—TVs, beautiful décor, and every new thing that is advertised. And yet, their homes are empty of people—empty of babies and children, the true riches that we can take into eternity with us.

I think of God's words about Israel when they walked in their own ways, *"Israel is an empty vine, he brings forth fruit unto himself"* (Hosea 10:1). When we focus on ourselves and our own aspirations, we are empty. We have nothing to give to anyone else. We have nothing to take into eternity.

The word "empty" in this Scripture is *baqaq* and means "to empty, to depopulate." Isn't that interesting? This is what has been happening in the church over the last few decades. As people have turned away from God's truths to fill their lives with the pleasures of this world, they have depopulated the church. Thousands and thousands of godly children who God intended to come forth to bring God's light and salvation into the world are not here. Not only have we depopulated the church, but we have depopulated the land. In turning from God's ways, we have become empty.

Other translations use the words **useless** (MLB), **worthless** (NLT), and **false** (Knox).

May God help us from wasting our lives on our own pursuits.

Prayer:

"Oh God, please keep me on your narrow way. I don't want to waste my life. Amen."

Affirmation:

Not my way, but God's way.

Day 91

Bypath Meadow

"A deceived heart has turned him aside"
(Isaiah 44:20).

Have you read the story of Pilgrim's Progress? If so, do you remember when Christian was tempted to turn into Bypath Meadow? Faithful and Christian were weary and the King's Way was rough and stony. They were tired and their feet ached. They came to a stile where the fence divided the King's Way from Bypath Meadow. Bypath Meadow was a smooth, grassy path instead of the rough stony one—but best of all, it ran right alongside the Way of the King. They wouldn't be going in the wrong direction. They really wouldn't be turning away and they would be able to jump back over the fence if it veered in the wrong direction.

They turned aside to the easy path. But, eventually a storm came and flooded the path. They were enveloped in darkness and could not find the way back to the King's Way. They fell asleep and were seized by Giant Despair and his cruel wife, Diffidence, who cruelly beat them and imprisoned them for some time, until God provided a way to escape.

This is how the enemy tempts us, too. We would never veer right away from the Lord. Of course we want to obey and follow Him. But we are often tempted to take the easy path. We are tired of the sacrifice, heartaches, and sleepless nights. We are tired of taking up our cross. We want it easy. We want everything to go our own way.

"Have another child? Help! Too much work. I want to take it easy. I want some rest." But, does it really make life easier? More children result in more blessings, more entertainment in the home, more diversity, more built-in helpers and built-in friends.

"Do I really have to stop eating all that sugar and all those carbs? I love them. They're my comfort food." They may be the desirable way, but not in the end!

"I'm overwhelmed with all this homeschooling. I can't take it any longer. I'm sending them back to public school." Sure, it's the easier way. But what about the ungodly influence on your children? What about the subtle humanist brainwashing? What about the ungodly friends they may make? How will it affect their destiny?

195

The easy path takes us further and further away from the truth. If we take the easy way in our family, we'll begin to take the easy way in other areas too. We'll begin to rely on government, rather than being a free people and taking responsibility for ourselves. We'll become weak and no longer a people of strength of character. And the long term result is bondage to dictatorship.

I was talking to a friend about a couple who are having marriage problems. "It's no use her going back to him until her heart wants to go back," my friend commented. "Oh no," I replied. "If she waits for her heart, she may never return!"

What does the Bible say in Jeremiah 17:9? *"The heart is deceitful above all things, and desperately wicked: who can know it?"* Our heart can so easily deceive us. We don't stay in a marriage because our heart is happy and wanting to stay. We stay in a marriage, or go back to a marriage if we have left it, because it is the right thing to do—because of obedience and commitment.

No wonder there is so much divorce today. Everyone wants to take Bypath Meadow. They want the easy way out. Everything revolves around self. "Poor me. He's not meeting my needs. He doesn't understand me." The excuses keep coming. But marriage is not all about "me." Marriage is forgetting about myself and concentrating on how I can serve my husband and family. It's commitment to my vows. It's not giving in to deceptive feelings, but sticking to the vision of building a godly generation. It continues in the face of hardship and frustration.

Marriage is more than two people. Marriage affects our children. It affects the extended family. It affects the church and everyone around us. It affects the generations to come—and eternity.

When we turn aside to the easy path, we enter into deviation, delusion, and deception. It's only when we get back on the King's Highway of truth that we will be safe, even though we may face challenges and difficulties.

Don't be deceived by the easy path.

Prayer:

"My God, please save me from being deceived. Save me from taking the easy path that looks good, but is not your way. Give me discernment to recognize the bypaths. Amen."

Affirmation:

I will not be deceived by the allurements of the easy way.

It Takes a Turning

"Behold, I will send you Elijah the prophet before the coming
of the great and dreadful day of the Lord; and he shall turn the heart of the
fathers to the children, and the heart of the children to their fathers,
lest I come and smite the earth with a curse"
(Malachi 4:5-6).

As we read this Scripture, we feel God's heart for families. God longs for the turning of the hearts to children. This should also be our prayer and longing.

We know this Scripture was fulfilled in the life of John the Baptist of whom it was said, *"He shall be filled with the Holy Ghost . . . And many of the children of Israel shall he **turn** to the Lord their God. And he shall go before him in the spirit and power of Elijah, **to turn the hearts of the fathers to the children,** and the disobedient to the wisdom of the just; to make ready a people prepared for the Lord"* (Luke 1:15-17).

God chose John the Baptist to prepare the people for the first coming of Jesus by turning the hearts of the fathers to the children. However, Jesus is coming a second time and the way must be prepared again. God is going to do it the same way, by turning the hearts of the fathers (and this also includes the mothers) back to the children. This issue is so important to the heart of God that He says that if it doesn't happen, He will smite the earth with a curse. This is not something we can take lightly.

God started this human race with the mandate, *"Be fruitful and multiply"* and He is going to finish it the same way. God hasn't changed His attitude toward children. He loves children. He calls them a blessing. When Jesus was on earth He embraced the children to Him and severely reprimanded those who turned them away. How can we be followers of God and yet have a different attitude about children than He does?

Are we on God's agenda or the devil's agenda? Truly it is time for God's people to turn back to His ways. Will we turn or will we have the curse?

Discernment Comes After Turning

Malachi 3:18 says, *"Then shall ye return, and discern between the righteous and the wicked, between him that serves God and him that serves him not."*

Do you notice that it is in returning that we will have understanding and discernment? While we continue to live according to our own agenda, we

197

often live in oblivion to what God really wants. It is when we turn from our own way and turn back to Him and obedience to His Word that we begin to understand truth we have not seen before. Discernment comes after turning.

It is time for us to turn from pride, stubbornness, prayerlessness, disobedience, mediocrity, passiveness, and following after the spirit of this world.

Jesus came to turn us away from ungodliness. *"God, having raised up his Son Jesus, sent him to bless you, in **turning away everyone of you from his iniquities**"* (Acts 3:26).

*"To open their eyes, and to **turn them from darkness to light**, and from the power of Satan unto God, that they may receive forgiveness of sins"* (Acts 26:18).

*"There shall come out of Zion the Deliverer, and shall **turn away ungodliness** from Jacob"* (Romans 11:26).

*"If thou **turn to the Lord thy God**, and shalt be obedient unto his voice . . . He will not forsake thee"* (Deuteronomy 4:30-31).

*"I thought on my ways, and **turned my feet unto thy testimonies**"* (Psalm 119:59).

*"Let us search and try our ways, and **turn again to the Lord**"* (Lamentations 3:40).

*"Turn thou us unto thee, O Lord, and **we shall be turned; renew our days as of old**"* (Lamentations 5:21).

Which way are we going to turn? This generation and future generations hinge upon our decision.

Prayer:
"Oh God please save me from being deceived. Help me to turn completely to you so that I will discern what is truth and what is your way. Amen."

Affirmation:
My heart is turned towards the Lord.

For Further Study On Turning Back To God, go to page 220.

Day 93

Dress for the Job

"Be dressed ready for service . . ."
(Luke 12:35 NIV).

What do you do when you get out of bed in the morning? Do you get dressed, or wander around in your robe or dressing gown?

I believe that what you do depends on your understanding of the task you have at hand. If you think your career of mothering and homemaking is insignificant, you may not be motivated to get dressed immediately. However, if you understand that you have the most important career in the nation, you will get dressed for the job. You will be up and ready to report to your Heavenly Employer.

Does your husband ever go to work in his pajamas? What an embarrassment that would be! Does a business woman go to her office in her nightgown? Laughable! But what do you do? How do you go to your work?

You have a greater work that is waiting for you as soon as you get out of bed. It is your anointed, influential, and eternal career of motherhood. You have heavenly employment! God himself has employed you to keep your home and raise the children He has given you to be mighty in His kingdom. This is no mean task. Nor is it part-time work. It is more important than the work of any politician. You are determining the destiny of the nation.

However, it does not happen automatically. It takes work! It takes work to run a home smoothly and keep it in order. It takes work to teach and raise children to become well-rounded, confident, and godly adults. To get "stuck in" to this great work, you have to dress for the job. No woman can work in her robe or dressing gown. When you get dressed, you are mentally geared for work. You are ready for service.

Can I encourage you to get dressed as soon as you get out of bed and be ready each morning for the service of the King? I love the rendering of Proverbs 31:1-18 in The Message, *"First thing in the morning, she dresses for work, rolls up her sleeves, ready to get started. She senses the worth of her work, is in no hurry to call it quits for the day."*

This kind of attitude brings a spirit of productivity to everyone in the home. A state of slothfulness and laziness should never be part of a godly home. Proverbs 31:27 in The Message says, "*She keeps an eye on everyone in her household and keeps them all busy and productive.*"

199

A mother's task is not only to be productive herself, but to keep each one of her children useful and industrious. It concerns me when I hear of children who are allowed to sleep in as long as they like and have not learned the habit of getting up early to start the day. It saddens my heart to see children, and especially older children, sitting around doing nothing! We must teach them to be productive. It is a mother's task to make sure that each child has their assigned tasks for the day and that they are motivated to engage in productive creativity.

Are you dressed for the job?

Prayer:

"Father, please help me to remember the enormity of the high calling that you have given to me. I want to be a faithful servant. Please help me not to slack on the job. Amen."

Affirmation:

I am reporting for duty each morning to the King of kings.

Cling to the Lord

*"Hezekiah . . . he did right in the sight of the Lord . . . he trusted in the Lord,
the God of Israel; so that after him there was none like him among all the
kings of Judah, nor among those who were before him. For he **clung to the
Lord**; he did not depart from following Him, but kept His commandments,
which the Lord had commanded Moses"*
(2 Kings 18:3, 5-6 NASB).

What a wonderful testimony to be written over a life. The Bible says that
there was no other king like Hezekiah. What was the secret of his success? He
clung to the Lord!

Where did he learn to cling to the Lord? I believe he learned it from his
mother, Abijah. Abijah was married to Ahaz, Hezekiah's father. Ahaz was a
wicked king, so wicked, that when he died they didn't even bury him in the
sepulchers of the kings of Israel. His greatest wickedness was that he followed
the way of the heathen nations around about him and actually *"burnt his children in the fire, after the abominations of the heathen"* (2 Chronicles 28:3).

Who were these children? Obviously they were some of the sons of Abijah. Dear, fellow mother, can you even begin to imagine the horror, the terror,
the torment, the anguish, the despair, the agony, and the dreadfulness (I can't
even find enough adjectives) that Abijah must have experienced as her precious little baby was ripped away from her loving arms and thrown into a fiery
pit? It is too painful to imagine. It would be enough to send her insane.

How did she survive? She must have clung to the Lord. The "God who is
Enough" was her comfort, her pillar, her rock, and her consolation. It was not
enough to pray. She was desperate. She had to cling to the Lord. She held fast
to the Lord and would not let Him go. This was her sanity.

Are you going through something in your life that you feel is too hard to
bear? Is your heart agonizing? Do more than say a little prayer; cling to the
Lord. Cry out to Him. Stay in His presence until you feel His loving arms
around you. As you draw near to Him, He will draw near to you. He will heal
your broken heart. He will keep your mind sound.

Do you have a problem that you don't know how to solve? Cling to the
Lord. Hold fast to the Lord until you receive His answer. Don't be swayed by
worldly answers but wait for His word to you.

Do you feel that you can hardly bear another moment in your marriage? Can you imagine the heartache Abijah endured as she lived with a man who threw her baby into the fire? Or maybe more than one baby? Dear one, cling to the Lord. Put your trust in the Lord. Have patience and wait for Him. God will work on your behalf, as you trust in Him. He will work wonders in you while you wait for His delivering power.

What was the fruit of Abijah's clinging to the Lord? She kept her sanity. She found her victory. She walked in dignity. And she raised a son who became a great king in Judah. She raised a godly man who influenced a nation for God. She taught him to "*cling to the Lord*" and that became the success of his life and his reign as one of the greatest kings of Judah. And Abijah's name is recorded in the Scriptures as a mother and powerful influence of a godly king.

Deuteronomy 13:4 NASB, "*You shall follow the Lord your God and fear Him; and you shall keep His commandments, listen to His voice, serve Him and **cling to Him**.*"

Deuteronomy 30:20, "***Cleave unto Him***: *for He is thy life, and the length of thy days.*" Read also Deuteronomy 10:20; 11:22; Joshua 22:5; 23:8 and Acts 11:23.

Cling to the Lord. He only is your deliverance.

Prayer:

"Dear Father, teach me to cling to you. Every other cistern leaks. You are the only one who can support me and hold me. I will cling to you. I will not let you go. I will hang on to you because you are my Source, my Life, my Hope, my Comfort, my Consolation, my Rock, and my faithful God. Amen."

Affirmation:

"The storm may roar about me,
My heart may low be laid;
But God is round about me,
And can I be dismayed?"
~ Anna L. Waring

Day 95

The Saddest Question!

"Knowest thou not that the Philistines are rulers over us?"
(Judges 15:11).

These are the words that the men of Judah said to Samson when the Philistines were after him. I think they are the saddest words I have ever read. God had given the land to the children of Israel. It belonged to them by the oracles and promises of God. It had been promised to them from the time of Abraham, Isaac, and Jacob. Under the leadership of Joshua, the land had been conquered and belonged to the children of Israel.

But now, years later, because they had turned away from the Lord, they had been taken over again by the Philistines. These men of Judah were so deceived that they actually believed that the Philistines were there rulers! They had become servants! Victims!

This was what they were experiencing, but they had forgotten the truth! The real truth was that the land belonged to them by God-given mandate! They were deceived! Over the years, their minds had been slowly seduced and now a new generation had grown up believing a lie!

Why are these such sad words? Because they are indicative of our situation today. America was founded on holiness and God's principles as the Pilgrims walked humbly before God and our founding fathers framed a godly constitution. But, now the humanists, abortionists, and socialists are ruling over us! This is not how it's meant to be.

It is so easy to be brain-washed by the media and humanist philosophy, isn't it? It can become part of our lives without our even realizing it. May we wake up to realize that the "Philistines" are not meant to be our rulers!

Samson did not give into the lie. He was only one lone voice but he defied the Philistines. He defeated the Philistines and became a judge over Israel for 20 years.

I am always challenged by Romans 3:4, *"Let God be true, but every man a liar."* I often ask myself, "Am I prepared to stand for God's truth even if everyone else is doing and saying something different?" The way of the majority is not always the right way. It is only God's way that is right, even if it is the narrow way and few are following it.

May God give us discernment. May we see clearly through all lies and deception. May God give us courage to stand for truth and walk in the light in the midst of darkness. May we not only put on our armor to protect ourselves from the onslaughts of the enemy but may God give us courage to be on the offensive—to use our sword, the truth of the Word of God, against the deceptions of the enemy.

Sometimes the "enemy" looks too big and we feel very insignificant. We may not be able to fight the big battle, but we can fight the little battles that we face from day to day. Little by little, we can win the victory. Sign petitions for godliness. Always stand up for the truth when talking with people from day to day. Never let deception go unchallenged.

Prayer:
"Oh God, please save me from being deceived. Your Word says that in the end time even the elect will be deceived. I don't want to be one of the deceived ones. I want to hear your voice. I want to walk in your truth. I want to discern between truth and error. Please sharpen my spiritual eyes and ears that I will not believe a lie."

Affirmation:
"Who is the liar that said a mother's role is inferior?"

A Poem to Read:
Keep Standing Strong
Go to page 224.

※⟨○⟩※

My Highest Purpose

Part 1

"Even everyone who is called by my name, whom I have created for my glory; I have formed him, yes, I have made him"
(Isaiah 43:7).

These wonderful words were spoken to Israel and they will be fulfilled in God's covenant people. However, they also speak to us who have been brought into God's family by the blood of Jesus that was shed for our sins. Before we can accomplish all that God has for us, we must first know His basic purpose for our lives. What is His purpose?

1. We were created for His glory (Isaiah 43:9).

Isn't this amazing? You were actually created to reveal God's glory. This gives wonderful meaning to life, doesn't it?

Look at 1 Corinthians 6:19-20, *"What? Know ye not that your body is the temple of the Holy Spirit which is you, which ye have of God, and ye are not your own. For ye are bought with a price: therefore glorify God in your body, and in your spirit, which are God's."* Read also 2 Corinthians 6:16.

Not only are we to glorify God by revealing a gentle and quiet spirit, but we are to glorify God in our body. We cannot align ourselves with "a woman's right to choose" because it is God's right to choose. Our life is not our own. Our body is not our own. It was made for His glory. How can a lawnmower give glory to its maker? By functioning as the designer planned it. How can a sewing machine give glory to its maker? By working according to the way it was designed. When it breaks down, it certainly doesn't glorify its maker. The designer gets a bad name!

In the same way, we give glory to God in our body by keeping it in good health and working order so that it can function according to the glorious way our Creator designed us. We do not glorify God by cutting off some function of the body that He has designed and created. Sadly, many do this today by sterilization. The Living Bible says, *"God has bought you with a great price. So use **every part** of your body to give glory back to God, because He owns it."* I am sure that "every part" means every part, don't you?

But, there is more yet! God says that our body is the temple of the Holy Spirit. The Greek word for "temple" is not *hieron* which represents the whole temple, but it is *naos* which refers to the Holy of Holies, the place where God's presence dwelt! This is too incredible! God wants your body to be a dwelling place for His presence so He can be revealed and glorified in this earth. The Knox translation says, "*Surely you know that your bodies are the shrines of the Holy Spirit, who dwells in you . . . glorify God by making your bodies the shrines of His presence.*"

When Jesus died, the thick veil hiding the Holy of Holies from the eyes of man was torn apart. God has now chosen the human body to be His *naos* where He dwells. He is no longer confined to one temple but dwells in *naos* dwelling places all over the world. This is how God is able to fill the earth with His glory—every believer a holy place for the indwelling of His presence so He can walk, live, and be revealed all over the earth—in every body, every home, every city, and every nation! What a revelation.

And think of this. The more children that we bring into this world, the more bodies there are for God to fill with His presence. Therefore the more of God's ways—His light, truth, love, and righteousness will fill the earth!

We must remember that God cannot fill our *naos* unless the blood is shed. The high priest could not enter that sacred place without the blood. The blood makes the way for God's presence in our lives. Live in the cleansing of the blood as He forgives you of the sins you confess to Him. Live under the protection of the blood as you acknowledge the power of the blood of Jesus to save you and deliver you.

Prayer:

"Dear Living God, please help me to comprehend your amazing purpose for my life, that my body is a sacred place for your presence. Please cleanse me from every evil sin in my life that I will truly be a holy temple to reveal your glory in this world. Help me to reveal your glory in my home, in my kitchen, and in my daily relationships and wherever I walk. Amen."

Affirmation:

Wherever I walk and every time I open my mouth, I have the opportunity to reveal God's glory.

My Highest Purpose

Part 2

"This people I have formed for myself; they shall declare my praise"
(Isaiah 43:21).

Not one of us is here on this earth by chance. God has purpose for our existence. He created and formed us for Himself. More than this, He loves us. Even more than this, He redeemed us. And more than this again, He has called us and chosen us in Him before the foundation of the world. Read Isaiah 43:1, 4, 7; 44:1, 2, 22, 23; Ephesians 1:4; 2:10 and 2 Timothy 1:9. When we understand this truth, there is no room for disillusionment or discontentment with life. It is the enemy of our souls who tells us that we are "good for nothing" or that life is not worth living.

Let's continue looking at the specific things for which God has created us . . .

2. We were created for God Himself (Isaiah 60:21).

We were not created for our own pleasure but for God's pleasure. Revelation 4:11 tells us that everything that God created was created for His pleasure. That includes us! The J.B. Phillip's translation of 1 Corinthians 6:19 reminds us, *"You are not the owner of your body."*

This takes a lot of the frustration out of life. We understand our purpose. We are not here to live for ourselves, but to bring pleasure and delight to the One who created us. What greater purpose could we find in life than to please our Creator and Redeemer? The Westminster Shorter Catechism says, "Man's chief end is to glorify God, and to enjoy Him forever."

When you wake in the morning, tell God, "Thank you that you created me for your pleasure. Here I am, Lord. I am available to serve you today. I want my life to bring pleasure to you." This purpose affects every moment and every aspect of your life. As you bring pleasure to your husband and your family in your home, you will also bring pleasure to the One who created you for this task.

God calls our children the work of His hands too, and it is important to remember that they also were born for His pleasure. Isaiah 29:23 says, *"For when he sees his children, the work of my hands, in his midst, they will sanctify my name . . . and will stand in awe of the God of Israel."* Only God can create a life, each one different than anyone else who has ever lived, each one with a different personality and gifts. When we see each one of our children growing in the Lord and honoring Him, it causes us to praise and stand in awe of Him. Every newborn baby is the exquisite work of God's hands and renews the face of the earth with the presence of God. Read Psalm 139:13-16 and 104:30.

The Living Bible and the New Living Translation give an interesting light on this Scripture, *"When they see the surging birth rate and the expanding economy, then they will fear and rejoice in my name . . . and stand in awe of Him."*

Prayer:

"Oh Lord, help me to become more and more aware of the glorious truth that I am created for your pleasure. You created me for your enjoyment and fellowship. Please help me to bring joy to you in every aspect of my life. Amen."

Affirmation:

I am created for God's pleasure!

Day 98

My Highest Purpose

Part 3

"Remember these, O Jacob and Israel; for you are my servant;
O Israel, you will not be forgotten by me!"
(Isaiah 44:21).

We continue discovering God's purposes for our lives . . .

3. We were created to show forth His praise (Isaiah 43:21b).

The words "show forth," besides meaning "to make known and to celebrate" also mean, "to inscribe." This same word was used for scribes. This means that in everything we say, write, and do, we are to make His praise known.

4. We were created to be His witnesses (Isaiah 43:10-13 and 44:8).

God's purpose for Israel was to witness to the world that God was the only true God. This is also our task. We are His representatives, His ambassadors, and His witnesses on this earth to show that He is the only true God and Savior in the earth. We are to declare His truth, His ways, and the knowledge of Him to the world. Of course, we start with our family! Every day we reveal to our children what God is like.

5. We were created to serve (Isaiah 44:21 and 49:3).

We were born to serve. To serve is God-like. Satan refused to serve in the heavenly realm and instead rose up in pride. Because of this he was cast out of heaven. Milton expresses Satan well in Paradise Lost . . .

"And in my choice
To reign is worth ambition though in hell:
Better to reign in hell, than serve in Heav'n."

Satan still tries to instill his anti-serving spirit in us today. It's helpful to remember that when we resist serving, we fall into Satan's willful ways.

Jesus Himself did not come to be served, but to serve. In fact, Jesus died, not only to save us from our sins, but also to save us from our selfish instinct that tries to rule our lives. 2 Corinthians 5:15 says, *"He died for all, that they which live should not henceforth live unto themselves, but unto him which died for them, and rose again."*

We often think of serving as servitude, but servitude is when we are made to serve, or when we do it grudgingly. We have joy when we willingly serve. It is God's purpose for us. I love the song we used to sing in New Zealand, "If you want to be great in God's kingdom, learn to be the servant of all!"

How can you serve God in your daily life? You serve Him by serving your husband and family. You serve Him when you are cleaning, cooking, and tending to your children and baby. When you serve in your home, you are actually serving the Lord. Every mundane task is a service to the Lord. 1 Corinthians 10:31 reminds us, "*Therefore, whether you eat or drink, or whatever you do, do all to the glory of God.*"

You serve God by serving one another. You serve Him by serving the poor and the "*least of the brethren*" (Matthew 25:31-46). When one of Mother Teresa's novices was ministering to one of the destitute, one who was repulsive to look at, or one whose stench was nauseating, she would often take the novice's hand. With the palm out-stretched, she would fold the fingers and thumb back into the palm one by one as she spoke these five words, "*You did it to Me.*"

Prayer:

"Lord, please help me to remember that serving is a godly attribute and that when I serve I am revealing your life. Help me to be full of joy as I serve in my home. Amen."

Affirmation:

To serve is greatness.

Day 99

The Door of Hope

"Blessed be the God and Father of our Lord Jesus Christ, which according to his abundant mercy has begotten us again unto a lively (living) hope by the resurrection of Jesus Christ from the dead"
(1 Peter 1:3).

Do you feel as though you are in a dungeon of despair? Maybe your marriage is in a mess. Maybe your children are out of control. Perhaps you feel as though you can't cope any longer.

Let me tell you a secret. There is a way out of the dungeon of despair! There is a door through which you can walk out! It is called the door of HOPE!

Hosea 2:15 says, *"And I will give her the valley of Achor for a DOOR OF HOPE: and she shall sing there, as in the days of her youth."*

Hope is a door that lets you out of your dungeon. While you look around at the mess you are in, your despair will engulf you. Instead, look up, dear mother. Believe me, there is a way out. You just have to turn the key of hope and you can walk out.

1 Peter 1:3 tells us that we have been born again to experience a living hope—a life of hope! E. Stanley Jones tells the story of a factory worker who testified that before he found Christ he wore his shoes out at the heels, but after he was born again, he wore them out at the toes! His life was tipped forward into expectancy.

What does this word "hope" really mean? The full meaning of this Greek word is as follows:

An energizing principle!
A spontaneous overflowing spirit of optimism!
A looking ever on the bright side of things!
A looking forward to only that which is good!
Expecting continued blessing and joy!
Exuberant hopefulness, leaving us no room for worry!
Believing that God is going to do something good!
Confident expectation!

How about that for a meaning? Is this the kind of life you are living? This is the life that Jesus died to bring you into!

Instead of groveling in your despair, start confessing out loud that God is a good God. Confess that He is going to do good things in your marriage, in your husband's life, in your life, in your home, and in each one of your children. Fill your home with confident, believing, and positive words. I know this is easier to say than do! You have to do it by faith, not because you feel like it.

Confess the words of Philippians 1:6 as you pray for your husband and your children: *"Being confident of this very thing, that he which hath begun a good work in you will perform it until the day of Jesus Christ."* Did God begin a good work in your husband? Don't despair because he is not walking as he should now. Come before the Lord and claim the promise that God will continue to perform His good work in him and that He will not stop until the day that Jesus comes.

When you speak words of hope, they will open the door into a life of hope! And you will start to sing again!

Holmes writes, "With eyes turned upward, whence her help descends, Hope waits EXPECTING till the tempest ends."

Come on now . . . don't stay in your valley of despair. Open the door of hope. Confess your trust in the Lord. Speak words of hope and things will change. Your circumstances may not change, but you will change! And that's the miracle.

My prayer for you is found in Romans 15:13, *"Now the God of hope fill you with all joy and peace in believing, that you may abound in hope, through the power of the Holy Ghost."*

Prayer:

"Oh God of Hope, thank you that you have redeemed me from the kingdom of darkness into a life of hope. Renew a spirit of hope in me again today. Let it bubble up inside me and overflow from me. I thank you that you are a good God and you are working everything out in my life for your highest purposes. I thank you for the good things you are doing in my life. I thank you for the good things you are doing in my husband's life and in my children's lives. I thank you that you are going to keep working in our lives until we see you face to face. Amen."

Affirmation:

"Though at times my spirit fails me,
And the bitter teardrops fall,
Though my lot is hard and lonely,
Yet I hope—I hope through all."
~ Mrs. Norton

Enrich Your Home

"Encourage one another daily"
(Hebrews 3:13).

God has blessed us as women with the ability to be sensitive to the needs around us. We sense when those in our family are in low spirits or need lifting up and encouraging. I believe this is one of the special privileges and responsibilities we have as a wife and mother—to be an . . .

Encourager—encouraging your husband and family each day.

Your husband is desperate for encouragement. He thrives on it. Encouragement will change his life and even his attitude toward you. Your children need encouragement. Encouragement is the rich soil in which they grow to their full development. We must give it daily, and even more than once a day. It should become a habit that flows from our lips. But more than an Encourager, you are also to be an . . .

Enricher—making your home richer each new day

This word means "to make richer." Is your home filled with love and the joy of the Lord? Make it richer with more love. Perhaps there is no loving atmosphere in your home. Start filling it up with love. It won't happen unless you do it. You are the Enricher, remember. You are the one who makes your home richer with all good things.

As you catch the vision to be the Encourager and Enricher of your home, you can also become an . . .

Enabler—enabling your children to reach their full destiny.

Endearer—endearing your family to each another.

Enhancer—enhancing the atmosphere of love and joy in your home.

Enlarger—enlarging your heart to the needs of your family, and maybe an orphan or two.

Enlightener—giving understanding and enlightenment of the ways of God to your children.

Enlivener—making your home alive with the presence of God.

Ennobler—training your children to be honorable and noble in all things.

Enthraller—enthralling your children with new ideas, creativity, and the wonders of God's creation.

Enthuser—enthusing your children to be ardent for God.

Entertainer—keeping your children happy and productive.

Enticer—enticing your children into the joy of prayer and reading God's living Word.

Enveloper—wrapping your children around with protection and love.

Envisioner—giving vision and hope to each member of the family.

Energizer—releasing the spirit of work and creativity in the home.

Engraver—engraving the names of your children upon your heart in prayer (Exodus 28:29-30).

Entreater—entreating your children to keep a straight course in the ways of God.

What an amazing vocation you have in your home!

Prayer:

"Lord, please show me ways that I can make my home richer in love and in the joy of your presence. Amen."

Affirmation:

I am making my home richer each day, not with material goods, but with lasting qualities.

Affirmations For You
To Pin Up In Your Home

The following are a few catchphrases, taken from the devotions and affirmations you have read in this book.

You may find it a blessing to write out specific ones, or type and print them in large letters from your computer. You can then pin them up in your kitchen, bedroom, or the best place to remind you. It's a great way to encourage you throughout the day and keep you on your toes.

Of course, the most important thing is to speak them out loud. What you speak out loud, you will put in to practice! You can read something, and affirm in your mind that it is a good idea, but it may not change you. When you speak it out loud, you will act on the words and begin to change.

For example, you are feeling tired and lying down on the couch, but tasks await you. You think about getting up, but it may not motivate you. Instead, confess out loud, "I'm getting off this couch right now to finish my job." When you speak, you will act.

Perhaps you are in a state of self-pity. Instead of realizing that what you are doing is ridiculous, speak out loud, "I'm going to stop crying right now and praise the Lord instead!" You'll soon be laughing!

You can change the phrases from week to week or from month to month. You can encourage your children to make positive confessions too!

I'm turning my sighs into hallelujahs!

I am a nurturer!

My home is an exciting place to live!

I am a liberated homemaker!

I am created for motherhood!

I am a covenant-keeper!

I am making my decisions in the light of eternity!

I am a nation builder!

I am above grumbling and self-pity!

My home is filled with miracles!

I am dangerous to the enemy!

I am a full-time missionary in my home!

I am raised to reign!

Sarah's daughter's don't panic!

I am looking down on my problems!

The tide always comes in again!

Jael's tent peg! (This reminds you to take authority over the enemy when he comes to tempt you or to steal from your marriage or home).

Out of my dungeon God lifts me up;
To wallow in self-pity I'd be a nut!

I am a joyful mother!

I am resting in the Lord today!

I look to God and worries cease,
Now my heart is filled with peace!

I am a family strengthener!

Doors are my praise opportunity!

The Lord is the Strength of my life!

We are a family who calls on the name of the Lord!

We are a smiling family!

I am created for God's pleasure!

I love working in my home!

I am an encourager!

My home is a sanctuary for God!

I am speaking only words of life today!

I am contented in my home!

I am proud to be called a mother!

I'm building my home with uplifting words.
To do anything else is utterly absurd!

I choose to praise instead of grumble!

I've had enough of being crabby,
I'm changing now to being happy!

I'm building a godly dynasty!

I love being a mother!

God is bigger than my problems!

I'm training an army for God!

God's timing is perfect!

I am investing in eternal riches!

I am the enricher of my home!

Always at the top, and never at the bottom!

I live in the ascended state!

Positive things in my home don't just happen. I have to make them happen!

Further Information and Study

Days 34 and 75

The following are further Scriptures to read about receiving instruction. These Scriptures will be a blessing to you and also your children. Many of them make great memory verses.

Proverbs 1:5, *"A wise man will **hear**, and will increase learning; and a man of understanding shall attain unto wise counsels."*

Proverbs 1:8, *"My son, **hear** the instruction of thy father, and forsake not the law of thy mother."*

Proverbs 4:1, *"**Hear**, ye children, the instruction of a father, and attend to know understanding."*

Proverbs 8:33, *"**Hear** instruction, and be wise, and refuse it not."*

Proverbs 12:15, *"He that **hearkens** unto counsel is wise."*

Proverbs 13:1, *"A wise son **hears** his father's instruction: but a scorner heareth not rebuke."*

Proverbs 15:31-32, *"The **ear that hears** the reproof of life abides among the wise. He that refuses instruction despises his own soul: but he that **hears** reproof gets understanding."*

Proverbs 19:20, *"**Hear** counsel, and receive instruction, that thou mayest be wise in thy latter end."* (Proverbs 29:15)

Proverbs 22:17, *"**Bow down thine ear, and hear** the words of the wise, and apply thine heart unto my knowledge."*

Proverbs 23:19, *"Hear thou, my son, and be wise."*

Proverbs 23:22, *"**Hearken** unto (hear) thy father that begat thee, and despise not thy mother when she is old."*

Ecclesiastes 5:1, *"**Be more ready to hear**, than to give the sacrifice of fools."*

Ecclesiastes 7:5, *"It is better to **hear** the rebuke of the wise, than for a man to hear the song of fools."*

Isaiah 43:9, *"Let them **hear**, and say, It is truth."*

Jeremiah 5:21, *"Hear now this, O foolish people, and without understanding; which have eyes, and see not; which have ears, and hear not."*

Ezekiel 40:4, *"Behold with thine eyes, and **hear** with thine ears, and set thine heart upon all that I shall show thee."*

Revelation 2:7, *"He that hath an ear, let him **hear** what the Spirit saith unto the churches."*

Proverbs 1:7, *"Fools despise wisdom and instruction."*

Proverbs 6:2-24, *"Reproofs of instruction are the way of life to keep thee from the evil woman…"*

Proverbs 9:8-9, *"Reprove not a scorner, lest he hate thee: rebuke a wise man, and he will love thee. Give instruction to a wise man, and he will be yet wiser teach just man, and he will increase in learning."*

Proverbs 10:8, *"The wise in heart will receive commandments."*

Proverbs 10:17, *"He that refuseth reproof erreth."*

Proverbs 12:1, *"Whoso loveth instruction loveth knowledge: but he that hateth reproof is brutish."*

Proverbs 13:18, *"Poverty and shame shall be to him that refuseth instruction: but he that regardeth reproof shall be honored."*

Proverbs 15:5, *"A fool desipseth his father's instruction: but he that regardeth reproof is prudent."*

Proverbs 15:10, *"He that hateth reproof shall die."*

Proverbs 17:10, *"A reproof entereth more into a wise man than a hundred stripes into a fool."*

Proverbs 19:25, *"Reprove one that hath understanding, and he will understand knowledge."*

Proverbs 21:11, *"When the wise is instructed, he receiveth knowledge."*

Proverbs 23:12, *"Apply thine heart unto instruction, and thine ears to the words of knowledge."*

Jeremiah 5:3-4, *"They have refused to receive correction… Therefore I said, Surely these are poor; they are foolish: for they know not the way of the Lord, nor the judgment of their God."*

Jeremiah 17:23, *"But they obeyed not, neither inclined their ear, but made their neck stiff, that they might not hear, nor receive instruction"* (22:33; 35:13).

WHAT IS GOD'S ATTITUDE TOWARD THE HUMBLE?
God cuts off the tongue that speaks proud things
*"The Lord shall **cut off** the tongue that speaks proud things: who have said, With our tongue will we prevail; our lips are our own: who is lord over us?"* (Psalm 12:3-4).

God cannot tolerate the proud
*"Him that hath a high look and a proud heart **will not I suffer**"* (Psalm 101:5 and Isaiah 2:11).

God resists the proud
*"God **resists** the proud"* (James 4:6 and 1 Peter 5:5).

God keeps the proud at arm's length
*"Though the Lord be high, yet hath he respect unto the lowly: but the proud he **knoweth afar off**"* (Psalm 138:6).

God hates pride
*"These things doth the Lord **hate**: a proud look"* (Proverbs 6:16-17).

God sees pride as an abomination
*"Every one that is proud in heart is an **abomination** to the Lord: though hand join in hand, he shall not be unpunished"* (Proverbs 16:5).

God sees pride as sin
*"A high look, and a proud heart is **sin**"* (Proverbs 21:4).

God brings down the proud
*"The lofty looks of man shall be humbled, and the haughtiness of men shall be bowed down… For the day of the Lord of hosts shall be upon every one that is proud and lofty, and upon every one that is lifted up; and he shall be **brought low**… And the loftiness of man shall be **bowed down**, and the haughtiness of men shall be **made low**"* (Isaiah 2:11-17). Read also Isaiah 3:16-24; 5:15; 10:33 and Proverbs 16:18.

WHAT IS GOD'S ATTITUDE TOWARD THE HUMBLE?

God exalts the humble (in due time)
"He that shall humble himself shall be exalted" (Matthew 23:12; Luke 14:11; 18:14; 1 Peter 5:6).

God gives grace to the humble
"He giveth grace unto the lowly" (Proverbs 3:34 and 1 Peter 5:5).

God lifts up the humble
"Humble yourselves in the sight of the Lord, and he shall lift you up" (James 4:10). Read also Psalm 147:6.

God saves the humble
"He shall save the humble person" (Job 22:29). Read also Psalm 34:18; 76:9 and 149:4.

God gives joy to the humble
"The meek also shall increase their joy in the Lord" (Isaiah 29:19).

God hears the cry of the humble
"Lord, thou hast heard the desire of the humble" (Psalm 10:17 and Psalm 9:12).

God dwells with the humble
"For thus saith the high and lofty One that inhabits eternity, whose name is Holy; I dwell in the high and holy place, with him also that is of a contrite and humble spirit, to revive the spirit of the humble, and to revive the heart of the contrite ones" (Isaiah 57:15).

God revives the humble
"To revive the spirit of the humble and to revive the heart of the contrite ones" (Isaiah 57:15b).

God rewards the humble
Jesus said, *"Whosoever therefore shall humble himself as this little child, the same is greatest in the kingdom of heaven"* (Matthew 18:4).

God turns away his wrath from the humble
"Notwithstanding Hezekiah humbled himself for the prid4 of his heart, both he and the inhabitants of Jerusalem, so that the wrath of the Lord came not upon them in the days of Hezekiah" (2 Chronicles 32: 26). Read also 1 Kings 21:29; 2 Chronicles 12:6-7, 12 and 33:12-13.

God respects the humble
"Though the Lord be high, yet hath he respect unto the lowly" (Psalm 138:6).

God looks to the humble
"But to this man will I look, even to him that is poor and of a contrite spirit, and trembleth at my word" (Isaiah 66:2).

God guides the humble
"The meek will he guide in judgment: and the meek will he teach his way" (Psalm 25:9).

God will cause the meek to inherit the earth
"The meek shall inherit the earth" (Psalm 37:11 and Matthew 5:5).

Day 52
The following are more Scriptures for you to study regarding God being a God of fullness.

*Everyone involved in the birth of Jesus was **filled** with the Holy Spirit* (Luke 1:15; 41; 67 and 2:40).

*The early church saints were **filled** with the Holy Spirit* (Acts 2:2-4; 4:8-10; 4:31; 6:3-5, 8; 7:55; 9:17-18; 11:22-24; 13:9-11 and 13:52).

*God is **full** of compassion* (Psalm 78:38; 86:15; 111:4; 112:4 and 145:8).

*The earth is **full** of the goodness of the Lord* (Psalm 24:1; 33:5; 50:12; 89:11; 119:64 and 1 Corinthians 10:26).

*The earth will be **full** of the glory of the Lord* (Numbers 14:21; Psalm 72:19; Isaiah 6:3; 11:9 and Habakkuk 2:14; 3:3).

*The earth will be **full** of the knowledge of the Lord* (Isaiah 11:9).

*God loves to **fill** us with food* (Leviticus 25:19; Deuteronomy 6:10-12; 8: 10-14; 11:14-15; 26:12; Nehemiah 9:25; Job 36:16b; Psalm 104:27-28; 1; 144:13; Proverbs 3:9-10; Isaiah 25:6, Joel 2:19 and Luke).

*God **filled** the earthly tabernacle* (Exodus 40:34-38).

*God **filled** the earthly tabernacle with His glory* (1 Kings 8:10-11; 2 Chronicles 5:13-14; 7:1-3; Isaiah 6:1; Ezekiel 10:3-4; 43:5 and 44:4).

Day 92

The following are more Scriptures about how God wants us to turn back to Him:

Exhortations to turn back to God
2 Chronicles 7:14; Job 36:10; Proverbs 1:23; Isaiah 44:22; Jeremiah 3:14a, 4:1; 19, 22; 18:11; 25:5-6; 36:3, 7; Ezekiel 14:6; 18:30-31; 33:11; Hosea 6:1; 12:6; 14:1-2; Joel 2:12-13; Zechariah 1:3-4 and Malachi 3:7.

We have a responsibility to exhort people to turn back to God
Jeremiah 23:22; 26:2-3; Ezekiel 33:7-9; Daniel 12:3; Malachi 2:6-7; Acts 14:15 and 26:16-18.

Prayers of turning back to God
1 Kings 8:35-36; 2 Chronicles 6:24-27; Psalm 80:3, 7, 19; 119:37; Jeremiah 31:18-19; Lamentations 5:21 and Hosea 14:1-2.

Examples of turning back to God
1 Kings 18:37-38; Malachi 3:18; 1 Thessalonians 1:9 and 1 Peter 2:25.

Examples of not turning away from God
1 Kings 15:4-5; 2 Kings 22:1-2; 23:25; Psalm 44:18 and Isaiah 50:5.

Examples of turning away from God
Leviticus 20:6; Numbers 14:43; Deuteronomy 31:18; Judges 8:33;1 Kings 11:1-11 and; 2 Chronicles 25:27; 29:6-8; Psalm 78:9, 41, 56-57; Proverbs 28:9; Isaiah 53:6; 44:20; 59:14-15; Jeremiah 2:21, 27; 3:10; 5:3; 11:9-11; 15:6-7; 23:14-15; 32:33; 50:6; Lamentations 1:8-9; Hosea 7:9-16; Amos 4:6, 9-11; Zephaniah 1:4-6; Haggai 2:17; Acts 7:39 and 2 Timothy 4:4.

Examples of turning away QUICKLY
Exodus 32:8; Deuteronomy 9:12, 16 and Judges 2:17.

Exhortations to turn from evil
Deuteronomy 5:32-33; 11:16-17; 26-28; 28:14; 29:18-20; 30:17-18; Joshua 1:7; 23: 6; 1 Samuel 12:20-21; 1 Kings 9:6-7; 2 Kings 17:13; 2 Chronicles 7:14; 19-20; Psalm 85:8; 125:5; Proverbs 4:27; Ezekiel 18:24-28; 33:12-20; 2 Timothy 3:5 and Hebrews 12:25.

God promises and blessings to us if we turn back to Him
Deuteronomy 4:30-31; 30:9-10; 1 Kings 18:37-38; 2 Chronicles 6:24-27, 37-39; 7:14; 7:19-20; 15:4; 30:6, 9; Nehemiah 1:9; Job 22:23; Isaiah 55:7; 59:20-21; Jeremiah 15:19-20; 18:7-10; 24:6-7; 26:2-3; Ezekiel 18:21-23; 33:14-16, 19; Joel 2:12-14; Zechariah 1:3 and Malachi 4:5-6.

Day 95

Here is a poem for you to read about STANDING UP FOR RIGHTEOUS-NESS IN THE NATION. I wrote it for my grandchildren but I think it will be a blessing to you too.

KEEP STANDING!
The morals of this world are going downhill,
Against God's Holy Word and His divine will,
No longer black and white, it's now mushy gray,
God's eternal absolutes many shun today.

Will you stand against this tide when others are crumbling?
Will you stand on God's Word when many are stumbling?
Will you stand against sin and the devil's deceptions?
Making no excuses or subtle exceptions?

Never be intimated, never be fooled...
Neutralized,
  Fraternized,
    Mediocre-ized
      Or your fire be cooled!

When there's no justice and only confusion,
And God's people are hiding their light in seclusion,
Will you rise up and be counted, open wide your mouth,
And proclaim God's truth to the north and the south?

Will you be strong in the Lord and the power of His might?
Always standing up for that which is right?
Rich in discernment, wisdom never ignored,
And walking daily in the fear of the Lord?

When you are tyrannized, never cower...
Patronized,
  Victimized,
    Or terrorized,
      Before the enemy never bow!

Will you stand the test when you are wronged and hurt?
When you are persecuted and treated like dirt?
Will you have backbone when the pressure comes on?
Or be a spineless jellyfish with purpose all gone?

Will you keep on standing if you're the only one?
Lifting up the name of Jesus, God's only Son?
Will you stand true now, holding on to the end?
No matter what it costs, God's truth to defend!

Never be wimpy or crumble at the knees...
Normalized,
  Traumatized,
    Luke-warmized,
      And the devil never appease!

Nancy Campbell

Made in United States
North Haven, CT
20 May 2023

36793886R00134